86. Chain Picot Edging 58
87. Littlest Scallop 59
88. Picot Ruffle 59
89. Wuffle Ruffle 59
90. Scallop Shell 60
91. Pearl Shell 60
92. Little Scallop 60
93. Ruffled Shell 61
94. Classic Shell 61
95. String of Pearls 61
96. Spike with Chain Loops 62
97. Spike and Chain Frill 62
98. Double Half Double with Picot 63
99. Chain and Zigzag 63
100. Crown Point 64

101. Shells and Columns

64

1. Single Crochet

Ch any number of sts plus 1.
Row 1 (RS) Work 1 sc in 2nd ch from hook and in each ch across. Turn.
Row 2 Ch 1 (counts as 1 sc), skip first sc, 1 sc in each sc across, end 1 sc in top of t-ch. Turn.
Rep row 2.

STITCH KEY
⬯ chain (ch)
+ single crochet (sc)

2. Single Crochet, Chain 1

Ch a multiple of 2 sts plus 2.
Row 1 (RS) Work 1 sc in 2nd ch from hook, *ch 1, skip next ch, sc in next ch; rep from * to end. Turn.
Row 2 Ch 1, 1 sc in first sc, *1 sc in next ch1 sp, ch 1; rep from * to last ch-1 sp, 1 sc in ch-1 sp, 1 sc in last sc. Turn.
Row 3 Ch 1, 1 sc in first sc, *ch 1, 1 sc in next ch-1 sp; rep from * to last 2 sc, ch 1, skip next sc, 1 sc in last sc. Turn.
Rep rows 2 and 3.

STITCH KEY
⬯ chain (ch)
+ single crochet (sc)

3. Back Loop Single Crochet

Ch any multiple of sts plus 1.
Row 1 (RS) Work 1 sc in 2nd ch from hook and in each ch across. Turn.
Row 2 Ch 1, 1 sc tbl in each sc across. Turn.
Rep row 2.

STITCH KEY

⊙ chain (ch)

┼ single crochet (sc)

single crochet through back loop (sc tbl)

4. Half Double Crochet

Ch any number of sts plus 2.
Row 1 (RS) Work 1 hdc in 3rd ch from hook and in each ch across. Turn.
Row 2 Ch 2, 1 hdc in each hdc across. Turn.
Rep row 2.

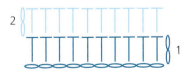

STITCH KEY

⊙ chain (ch)

T half double crochet (hdc)

5. Double Crochet

Ch any number of sts plus 3.
Row 1 (RS) Work 1 dc in 4th ch from hook and in each ch across. Turn.
Row 2 Ch 3 (counts as 1 dc), skip first dc, 1 dc in each dc across, end 1 dc in top of ch-3 t-ch. Turn.
Rep row 2.

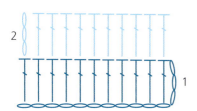

STITCH KEY
- chain (ch)
- double crochet (dc)

6. Solid Scallop

Ch a multiple of 6 sts plus 2.
Row 1 (RS) Work 1 sc in 2nd ch from hook, *skip 2 ch, 5 dc in next ch, skip 2 ch, 1 sc in next ch; rep from * across. Turn.
Row 2 Ch 3 (counts as 1 dc), 2 dc in first sc, *1 sc in center dc of next scallop, 5 dc in next sc; rep from *, end last rep 3 dc in last sc. Turn.
Row 3 Ch 1, 1 sc in first dc, *5 dc in next sc, 1 sc in center dc of next scallop; rep from *, end last rep 1 sc in top of t-ch. Turn.
Rep rows 2 and 3.

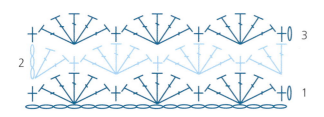

STITCH KEY
- chain (ch)
- single crochet (sc)
- double crochet (dc)

7. Wide Rib

Ch any multiple of sts plus 3.
Row 1 (RS) Work 1 dc in 4th ch from hook and in each ch across. Turn.
Row 2 Working through both lps across row, 1 sc in first st, insert hook in same st and draw up a lp, insert hook in next st and draw up a lp, draw last lp directly through 2 lps on hook, *insert hook in same st as last completed st, yo and draw up a lp, insert hook in next st and draw up a lp, draw last lp directly through 2 lps on hook; rep from * in each st across, work additional sl st in last st. Turn.
Row 3 Ch 3, 1 dc tbl in each st across. Turn.
Rep rows 2 and 3.

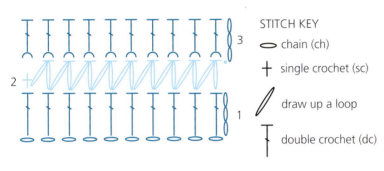

STITCH KEY
- chain (ch)
- single crochet (sc)
- draw up a loop
- double crochet (dc)
- double crochet through back loop (dc tbl)
- slip stitch (sl st)

8. Front Loop Double Crochet

Ch any number of sts plus 3.
Row 1 (RS) Work 1 dc in 4th ch from hook and in each ch across. Turn.
Row 2 Ch 3 (counts as 1 dc), skip first dc, double crochet through front loop (dcfl) in each st across, dc in top of t-ch. Turn.
Rep row 2.

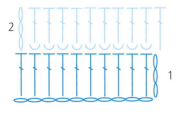

STITCH KEY
- chain (ch)
- double crochet (dc)
- double crochet through front loop (dcfl)

9. Puff Stripes

Ch a multiple of 4 sts plus 2.
Row 1 (RS) In 2nd ch from hook work puff st, 1 hdc in each ch to last ch, 1 puff st in last ch. Cut yarn and rejoin at beg of RS row.
Row 2 (RS) Ch 2, 1 puff st in first st, 1 hdc in each hdc to last st, 1 puff st in last st. Turn.
Row 3 (WS) Working very loosely, ch 1, 1 sc in each st across. Turn.
Row 4 (RS) Working very loosely, ch 1, 1 sc in first sc, *ch 3, skip 3 sc, 1 sc in next sc; rep from * to end. Turn.
Row 5 (WS) Working very loosely, ch 1, 1 sc in first sc, *3 sc in ch-3 sp, 1 sc in next sc; rep from * to end. Turn.
Row 6 (RS) Ch 2, puff st in first st, 1 hdc in each st to last st, 1 puff st in last st. Cut yarn and rejoin at beg of RS row.
Rep rows 2–6.

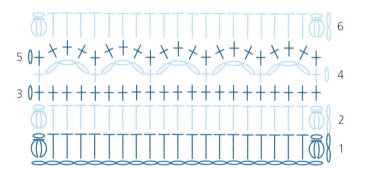

STITCH KEY
- ⌒ chain (ch)
- + single crochet (sc)
- T half double crochet (hdc)
- 🮲 puff stitch

10. Crochet Cable

Ch a multiple of 4 sts plus 3.
Row 1 (RS) Work 1 sc in 2nd ch from hook and in each ch across. Turn.
Row 2 Ch 3 (counts as 1 dc), *skip next sc, 1 dc in next 3 sc, yo, with hook in front of work, go back and insert hook from front to back into skipped st before the 3-dc group; loosely draw through a lp and bring it up to the height of the 3-dc group; yo and complete dc (cable st); rep from * across, end dc in last st. Turn.
Row 3 Ch 1, 1 sc in each dc across. Turn.
Rep rows 2 and 3.

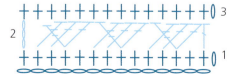

STITCH KEY
- ⌒ chain (ch)
- + single crochet (sc)
- T double crochet (dc)

11. Petite Popcorns

STITCH GLOSSARY
Popcorn In next sc [yo and draw up a lp] 5 times, yo and draw through all 5 lps on hook.

Ch a multiple of 3 sts plus 2.
Row 1 (RS) Work 1 sc in 2nd ch from hook and in each ch across. Turn.
Row 2 Ch 1, 1 sc in first sc, *popcorn in next sc, 1 sc in each of next 2 sc; rep from * across. Turn.
Row 3 Ch 1, 1 sc in each st across. Turn.
Row 4 Ch 1, *1 sc each of next 2 sc, popcorn in next sc; rep from *, end 1 sc in last sc. Turn.
Row 5 Rep row 3.
Rep rows 2–5.

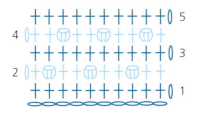

STITCH KEY
- chain (ch)
+ single crochet (sc)
popcorn

12. Alternating Ridge Pattern

Ch a multiple of 2 sts plus 1.
Row 1 (RS) Work 1 sc in 2nd ch from hook, *skip next ch, 2 sc in next ch; rep from *, end 1 sc in last ch. Turn.
Row 2 Ch 2, hdc in first st, *skip next st, 2 hdc in next st; rep from *, end hdc in last st. Turn.
Rows 3 and 4 Ch 1, 1 sc in first st, *skip next st, 2 sc in next st; rep from *, end sc in last st. Turn.
Rep rows 2–4.

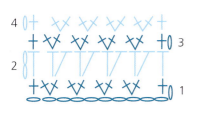

STITCH KEY
- chain (ch)
+ single crochet (sc)
T half double crochet (hdc)

13. Wave Pattern

Ch a multiple of 12 sts plus 5.

Row 1 (RS) In 6th ch from hook work [1 tr, ch 1] 3 times, skip 5 ch, 1 sc in next ch, *ch 1, skip 5 ch, in next ch work [1 tr, ch 1] 7 times, skip 5 ch, 1 sc in next ch; rep from * to last 6 ch, ch 1, in last ch work [1 tr, ch 1] 3 times, 1 tr in same ch. Turn.
Row 2 Ch 1, 1 sc in first tr, *ch 6, 1 sc in next sc, ch 6, skip 3 tr, 1 sc in next tr; rep from *, end last rep 1 sc in 4th ch of t-ch. Turn.
Row 3 Ch 1, 1 sc in first sc, *ch 6, 1 sc in next sc; rep from * across. Turn.
Row 4 Ch 1, 1 sc in first sc, *ch 1, in next sc work [1 tr, ch 1] 7 times, 1 sc in next sc; rep from * across. Turn.
Row 5 Ch 1, 1 sc in first sc, *ch 6, skip 3 tr, 1 sc in next tr, ch 6, 1 sc in next sc; rep from * across. Turn.
Row 6 Rep row 3.
Row 7 Ch 5 (counts as 1 tr and ch 1), in first sc work [1 tr, ch 1] 3 times, 1 sc in next sc, *ch 1, in next sc work [1 tr, ch 1] 7 times, 1 sc in next sc; rep from * to last sc, in last sc work [ch 1, 1 tr] 4 times. Turn.
Rep rows 2–7.

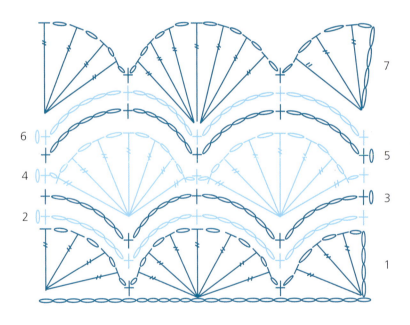

STITCH KEY

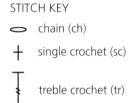

chain (ch)

single crochet (sc)

treble crochet (tr)

14. Pretty Ballerina

COLORS
A (deep blue), B (light pink), C (green), and D (purple)

With A, ch 4 and join with sl st in first ch to form ring.
Rnd 1 [1 sc, ch 3] 4 times in ring. Join with sl st to first sc.
Rnd 2 Sl st in ch-3 sp, ch 3 (counts as 1 dc), (2 dc, ch 3, 3 dc) in same sp, *[(3 dc, ch 3, 3 dc) in next sp] 3 times. Join with sl st to top of beg ch-3—4 corner ch-3 sps. Fasten off.
Rnd 3 With B and lp on hook, (1 sc, ch 3, 1 sc) in corner ch-3 sp, *ch 3, 1 sc between next 3rd and 4th dc, ch 3, (1 sc, ch 3, 1 sc) in next corner ch-3 sp; rep from *, end ch 3, 1 sc between next 3rd and 4th dc, ch 3. Join with sl st to first sc.
Rnd 4 Sl st in corner ch-3 sp, ch 3 (counts as 1 dc), (2 dc, ch 3, 3 dc) in same corner, *[3 dc in next ch-3 sp] twice**, (3 dc, ch 3, 3 dc) in next corner; rep from * twice more, then from * to ** once. Join with sl st to top of beg ch-3. Fasten off.
Rnd 5 With C and lp on hook, *(1 sc, ch 3, 1 sc) in corner ch-3 sp, [ch 3, 1 sc between next 3rd and 4th dc] 3 times, ch 3; rep from * to around. Join with sl st to first sc.
Rnd 6 Sl st in corner ch-3 sp, ch 3 (counts as 1 dc), (2 dc, ch 3, 3 dc) in same corner, *[3 dc in next ch-3 sp] 4 times**, (3 dc, ch 3, 3 dc) in next corner; rep from * twice more, then from * to ** once. Join with sl st to top of beg ch-3. Fasten off.

Rnd 7 With D and lp on hook, (1 sc, ch 7, 1 sc) in corner ch-3 sp, [ch 5, 1 sc between next 3rd and 4th dc] 5 times, *ch 5, (1 sc, ch 7, 1 sc) in next corner ch-3 sp, [ch 5, 1 sc between next 3rd and 4th dc] 5 times; rep from*, end ch 5. Join with sl st to first sc. Fasten off.

COLOR & STITCH KEY

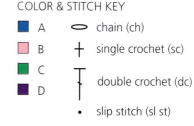

- A — chain (ch)
- B + single crochet (sc)
- C ╪ double crochet (dc)
- D • slip stitch (sl st)

15. Spring Medallion

COLORS
A (green) and B (yellow)

With A, ch 8 and join with sl st in first ch to form ring.
Rnd 1 (RS) Ch 6 (counts as 1 dc and ch 3), [1 dc, ch 3] 7 times in ring. Join with sl st to 3rd ch of beg ch-6—8 ch-3 sps. Fasten off.
Rnd 2 With B, sl st to first ch-3 sp, (ch 3, 3 dc) in same sp, *(ch 2, 4 dc) in next sp; rep from *, end ch 2. Join with sl st to top of beg ch-3. Fasten off.
Rnd 3 With A, sl st to first ch-2 sp, (ch 3, 5 dc) in ch-2 sp, *ch 3, 6 dc in next ch-2 sp, ch 1, 6 dc in next ch-2 sp; rep from *, end ch 3, 6 dc in ch-2 sp, ch 1. Join with sl st to top of beg ch-3. Fasten off.
Rnd 4 With B and lp on hook, sc in ch-1 sp, ch 3, *1 sc between 3rd and 4th dc of 6-dc group, ch 3, (2 dc, ch 2, 2 dc) in corner ch-3 sp, ch 3, 1 sc between 3rd and 4th dc of 6-dc group, ch 3**, 1 sc in ch-1 sp, ch 3; rep from * twice more, then from * to ** once. Join with sl st to first sc.
Rnd 5 Sl st to first ch-3 sp, ch 1, [3 sc in ch-3 sp] twice, *(1 sc between next 2 dc, 4 sc in corner ch-2 sp, 1 sc between next 2 dc), [3 sc in next ch-3 sp] 4 times; rep from *, end last rep [3 sc in ch-3 sp] twice. Join with sl st to first sc.
Rnd 6 *Ch 4, skip 1 sc, sl st in next sc; rep from * around, end last rep with ch 4, skip 1 sc. Join with sl st to 1st ch of beg ch-4. Fasten off.

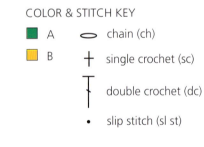

COLOR & STITCH KEY

- A
- B
- chain (ch)
- + single crochet (sc)
- double crochet (dc)
- • slip stitch (sl st)

16. Mme. Butterfly

COLORS
A (green), B (orange), C (light pink), D (purple), and E (yellow)

With A, ch 4 and join with sl st in first ch to form ring.
Row 1 (RS) [1 sc, ch 3] 3 times, 1 sc in ring. Do not join. Fasten off, turn.
Row 2 With B, sl st in first sc, ch 3 (counts as 1 dc throughout), 3 dc in first ch-3 sp, (3 dc, ch 3, 3 dc) in next sp for corner, 4 dc in last ch-sp. Fasten off, turn.
Row 3 With A and lp on hook, (1 sc, ch 3, 1 sc) between 1st and 2nd dc, ch 3, 1 sc between next 3rd and 4th dc, ch 3, (1 sc, ch 3, 1 sc) in corner sp, ch 3, 1 sc between next 3rd and 4th dc, ch 3, (1 sc, ch 3, 1 sc) between last dc and t-ch. Fasten off, turn.
Row 4 With C, sl st in first sc, ch 3, 3 dc in first ch-3 spc, [3 dc in next ch-3 sp] twice, (3 dc, ch 3, 3 dc) in corner sp, [3 dc in next ch-3 sp] 3 times, end 1 dc in last sc. Fasten off, turn.
Row 5 With D and lp on hook, (1 sc, ch 3, 1 sc) in first dc, [ch 3, 1 sc between next 3rd and 4th dc] 3 times, ch 3, (1 sc, ch 3, 1 sc) in corner sp, [ch 3, 1 sc between next 3rd and 4th dc] 4 times, ch 3, 1 sc in top of t-ch. Fasten off, turn.
Row 6 With E, sl st in first sc, ch 3, 3 dc in first ch-3 sp, [3 dc in next ch-3 sp] 4 times, (3 dc, ch 3, 3 dc) in corner sp, [3 dc in next ch-3 sp] 4 times, 3 dc in last ch-3 sp, 1 dc in last sc. Fasten off, turn.
Row 7 With A and lp on hook, (1 sc, ch 7, 1 sc) in first dc, [ch 5, 1 sc between next 3rd and 4th dc] 5 times, (ch 7, 1 sc, ch 7) in corner sp, [1 sc between next 3rd and 4th dc, ch 5] 5 times, (1 sc, ch 7, 1 sc) in last dc. Fasten off.

COLOR & STITCH KEY
- A
- B
- C
- D
- E
- chain (ch)
- single crochet (sc)
- double crochet (dc)
- slip stitch (sl st)

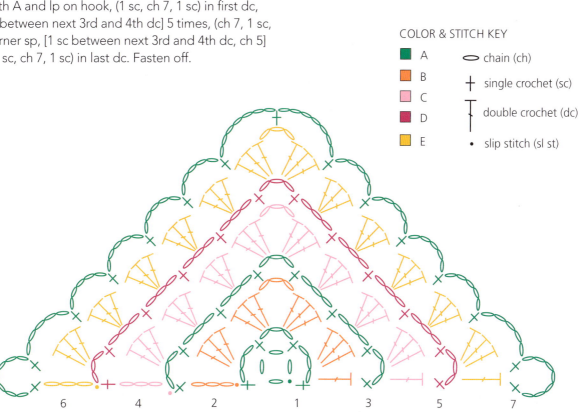

17. Radiant

STITCH GLOSSARY

CL2 (dc2tog) [Yo and insert hook into st, yo and draw up a lp through st, yo and draw through 2 lps on hook] twice, yo and draw through all 3 lps on hook.

CL3 (dc3tog) [Yo and insert hook into st, yo and draw up a lp through st, yo and draw through 2 lps on hook] 3 times, yo and draw through all 4 lps on hook.

COLORS

A (light pink), B (purple), and C (mauve/pink)

With A, ch 5 and join with sl st in first ch to form ring.
Rnd 1 Ch 3, CL2, [ch 3, CL3] 7 times in ring, end ch 3. Join with sl st to top of first cluster—8 clusters. Fasten off.
Rnd 2 With B, sl st in first corner ch-3 sp, ch 3 (counts as 1 dc), (2 dc, ch 3, 3 dc) in same ch-3 sp, *3 hdc in next ch-3 sp, (3 dc, ch 3, 3 dc) in corner ch-3 sp; rep from *, end 3 hdc in last ch-3 sp. Join with sl st to top of beg ch-3. Fasten off.
Rnd 3 With A, sl st in same place as joining, ch 1, 1 sc in next 2 sts, *(2 sc, ch 2, 2 sc) in next corner ch-3 sp, skip 1 dc, 1 sc in next 8 sts; rep from *, end last rep 1 sc in last 6 sts. Join with sl st to first sc. Fasten off.
Rnd 4 With B and lp on hook, 1 sc in first ch-2 sp, 1 sc in same sp, *1 sc in next 12 sc, 2 sc in corner ch-2 sp; rep from * around. Join with sl st to first sc. Fasten off.
Rnd 5 With C and lp on hook, 2 sc in first st of first corner, 2 sc in next corner st of same corner, *1 sc in next 12 sc [2 sc in next corner sc] twice; rep from * around, end 1 sc in last 12 sc. Join with sl st to first sc. Fasten off.

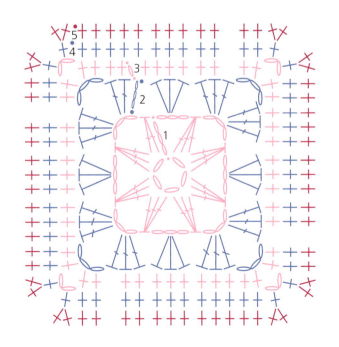

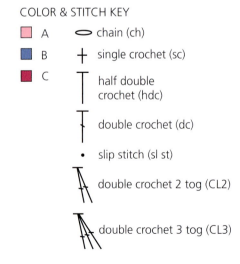

18. Pinwheel

STITCH GLOSSARY
CL3 (3-st Puff) [Yo and draw up a lp, yo and draw through 1 lp on hook] 3 times in same sp, yo and through all 7 lps.
CL4 (4-st Puff) [Yo and draw up a lp, yo and draw through 1 lp on hook] 4 times in same sp, yo and through all 9 lps.
Picot (3-ch) Ch 3, insert hook down through top of last tr and sl st.

Ch 6 and join with sl st in first ch to form ring.
Rnd 1 (RS) Ch 4 (counts as 1 dc and ch 1), [1 dc, ch 1] 11 times in ring—12 ch-1 sps. Join with sl st in 3rd ch of beg ch-4.
Rnd 2 Sl st into first ch-1 sp, (ch 3, CL3) in same sp, ch 2, *CL4 in next ch-1 sp, (ch 3, 1 tr in dc, ch 3) for corner, [CL4 in ch-1 sp, ch 2] twice; rep from *, end last rep CL4 in ch-1 sp, ch 2. Join with sl st to top of first puff st.
Rnd 3 Ch 1, 1 sc in same place as joining, *ch 2, skip next ch-2 sp, 4 dc in next ch-3 sp, ch 2, 1 tr in tr, picot, ch 2, 4 dc in next ch-3 sp, ch 2, skip next ch-2 sp, 1 sc in CL4; rep from *, end last rep 4 dc in last ch-3 sp, ch 2, skip last ch-2 sp. Join with sl st to first sc. Fasten off.

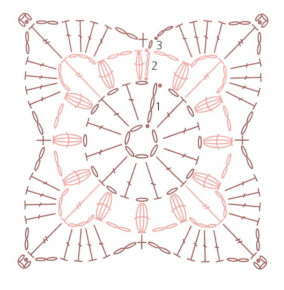

STITCH KEY

◯ chain (ch)

✚ single crochet (sc)

┬ double crochet (dc)

╤ treble crochet (tr)

• slip stitch (sl st)

◆ 3-st puff (CL3)

◆ 4-st puff (CL4)

⊙ picot

19. Tilted Cluster

STITCH GLOSSARY
CL2 (2-dc Cluster) [Yo and draw up a lp, yo and draw through 2 lps on hook] twice in same sp, yo and draw through all 3 lps on hook.
CL3 (3-dc Cluster) [Yo and draw up a lp, yo and draw through 2 lps on hook] 3 times in same sp, yo and draw through all 4 lps on hook.

COLORS
A (light pink), B (purple), and C (green)

With A, ch 4 and join with sl st in first ch to form ring.
Rnd 1 (RS) Ch 4 (counts as 1 dc and ch 1), [1 dc, ch 1] 11 times in ring. Join with sl st to 3rd ch of beg ch-4 —12 ch-1 sps. Fasten off.
Rnd 2 With B, sl st to a ch-1 sp, (ch 3, CL2) in same ch-1 sp, [ch 3, CL3 in next ch-1 sp] 11 times, ch 3. Join with sl st to top of CL2—12 clusters. Fasten off.
Rnd 3 With C and lp on hook, 1 sc in ch-3 sp, ch 5, [1 sc in ch-3 sp, ch 5] 11 times. Join with sl st to first sc. Fasten off.
Rnd 4 With B and lp on hook, 1 sc in first ch-5 sp, *ch 5, 1 sc in next ch-5 sp, ch 1, (5 dc, ch 3, 5 dc) in next ch-5 sp, ch 1**, 1 sc in next ch-5 sp; rep from * twice more, then from * to ** once. Join with sl st to first sc. Fasten off.

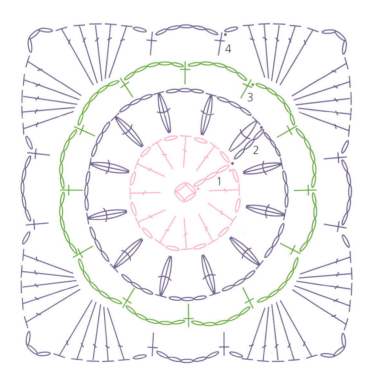

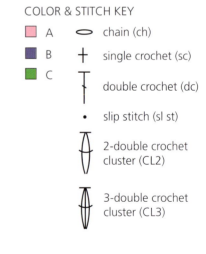

COLOR & STITCH KEY
- A
- B
- C
- chain (ch)
- single crochet (sc)
- double crochet (dc)
- slip stitch (sl st)
- 2-double crochet cluster (CL2)
- 3-double crochet cluster (CL3)

20. Helianthus

COLORS
A (green) and B (yellow)

With A, ch 6 and join with sl st in first ch to form ring.
Rnd 1 (RS) Ch 3 (counts as 1 dc), 15 dc in ring. Join with sl st to top of beg ch-3—16 dc. Fasten off.
Rnd 2 With B, sl st in top of joining, ch 5 (counts as 1 dc and ch 2), 1 dc in same place as joining, [ch 1, skip 1 dc, (1 dc, ch 2, 1 dc) in next dc] 7 times, end ch 1. Join with sl st in 3rd ch of beg ch-5.
Rnd 3 Sl st in first ch-2 sp, ch 3 (counts as 1 dc), (1 dc, ch 2, 2 dc) in same ch-2 sp, *ch 1, (2 dc, ch 2, 2 dc) in next ch-2 sp; rep from * around, ch 1. Join with sl st to top of beg ch-3.
Rnd 4 Sl st in next dc and first ch-2 sp, ch 4 (counts as 1 tr), 7 tr in same ch-2 sp, *1 sc in ch-1 sp, 8 tr in ch-2 sp; rep from * around. Join by inserting hook through ch-1 sp, then 1 sc in 4th ch of beg ch-4. Fasten off.

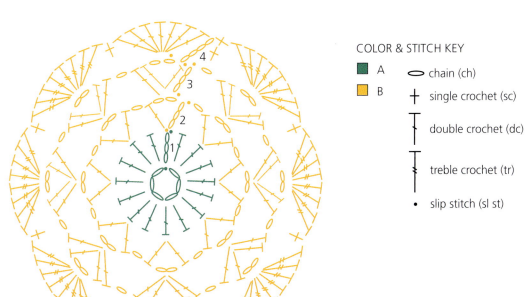

COLOR & STITCH KEY

- ■ A   ⬭ chain (ch)
- ■ B   ✚ single crochet (sc)
-         ┬ double crochet (dc)
-         ┳ treble crochet (tr)
-         • slip stitch (sl st)

21. Star Puff

STITCH GLOSSARY
CL2 (2-st Puff) [Yo and draw up a lp, yo and draw through 1 lp on hook] twice in same sp, yo and draw through all 5 lps on hook.
CL3 (3-st Puff) [Yo and draw up a lp, yo and draw through 1 lp on hook] 3 times in same sp, yo and draw through all 7 lps on hook.

COLORS
A (yellow) and B (green)

With A, ch 7 and join with sl st in first ch to form ring.
Rnd 1 (RS) Ch 1, 12 sc in ring. Join with sl st to first sc.
Rnd 2 Ch 3 (counts as 1 dc), 1 dc in next sc, [ch 3, 1 dc in next 2 sc] 5 times, ch 3. Join with sl st to top of beg ch-3 —6 ch-3 sps. Fasten off.
Rnd 3 With B, sl st in first ch-3 sp, ch 3 (counts as 1 dc), (CL2, ch 4, CL3) in same ch-3 sp, [ch 4, (CL3, ch 4, CL3) in next ch-3 sp] 5 times, ch 4. Join with sl st to top of CL2.
Rnd 4 Ch 1, (2 sc, ch 4, 2 sc) in first ch-4 sp, [(2 sc, ch 4, 2 sc) in next ch-4 sp] 11 times. Join with sl st to first sc. Fasten off.

COLOR & STITCH KEY
- A
- B
- chain (ch)
- single crochet (sc)
- double crochet (dc)
- slip stitch (sl st)
- 2-double crochet cluster (CL2)
- 3 double crochet cluster (CL3)

22. Half Star

STITCH GLOSSARY
CL2 (2-st Puff) [Yo and draw up a lp, yo and draw through 1 lp on hook] twice, yo and draw through all 5 lps on hook.
CL3 (3-st Puff) [Yo and draw up a lp, yo and draw through 1 lp on hook] 3 times, yo and draw through all 7 lps on hook.

COLORS
A (purple) and B (green)

With A, ch 7 and join with sl st in first ch to form ring.
Row 1 (WS) Ch 1, 8 sc in ring. Do not join. Turn.
Row 2 (RS) Ch 4 (counts as 1 dc and ch 1), skip first sc, [1 dc in next 2 sc, ch 3] twice, 1 dc in next 2 sc, ch 1, 1 dc in last sc. Fasten off.
Row 3 (RS) With B and lp on hook, (1 sc, ch 3, CL2) in first ch-1 sp, [ch 4, (CL3, ch 4, CL3) in next ch-3 sp] twice, ch 4, (CL3, ch 1, 1 dc) in last ch-1 sp. Fasten off.
Row 4 (RS) With B and lp on hook, (1 sc, ch 3, 2 sc) in first ch-3 sp at beg of row 3, *(2 sc, ch 3, 2 sc) in next ch-4 sp; rep from * 4 times more, end (2 sc, ch 3, 1 sc) in last ch-1 sp. Fasten off.

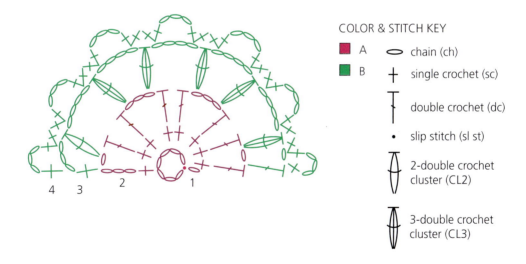

COLOR & STITCH KEY
- A
- B
- chain (ch)
- single crochet (sc)
- double crochet (dc)
- slip stitch (sl st)
- 2-double crochet cluster (CL2)
- 3-double crochet cluster (CL3)

23. Pansy

COLORS
A (green) and B (purple)

With A, ch 6 and join with sl st in first ch to form ring.
Rnd 1 (RS) Ch 3 (counts as 1 dc), 15 dc in ring. Join with sl st to top of beg ch-3—16 dc. Fasten off.
Rnd 2 With B, sl st in top of joining, ch 1, 1 sc in same place as joining, 1 sc in next dc, *(1 sc, ch 7, 1 sc) in next dc, 1 sc in next 3 dc; rep from *, end last rep 1 sc in last dc. Join with sl st to first sc.
Rnd 3 Ch 1, 1 sc in same place as joining, *skip 2 sc, 15 hdc in ch-7 sp, skip 2 sc, 1 sc in next sc; rep from *, end last rep, omitting 1 sc in next sc. Join with sl st to first sc.
Rnd 4 Sl st in first 5 hdc, ch 1, 1 sc in same st as last sl st, *ch 8, skip 5 hdc, 1 sc in next hdc, ch 6, skip (4 hdc, 1 sc, 4 hdc), 1 sc in next hdc; rep from *, end last rep, omitting 1 sc in next sc. Join with sl st to first sc.
Rnd 5 Ch 2, *(4 hdc, 3 dc, 4 hdc) in next ch-8 sp, 1 hdc in next sc, 6 hdc in next ch-6 sp, 1 hdc in next sc; rep from *, end last rep, omitting last 1 hdc in next sc. Join with sl st to first hdc. Fasten off.

COLOR & STITCH KEY

- ▪ A   ⚬ chain (ch)
- ▪ B   + single crochet (sc)
- T half double crochet (hdc)
- ⊤ double crochet (dc)
- • slip stitch (sl st)

24. Starlight

STITCH GLOSSARY
Picot (4-ch) Ch 4, sl st in 4th ch from hook.

Ch 7 and join with sl st in first ch to form ring.
Rnd 1 (RS) Ch 2 (counts as 1 sc), 11 sc in ring. Join with sl st to top of beg ch-2.
Rnd 2 Ch 4 (counts as 1 dc and ch 1), [1 dc in next sc, ch 1] 11 times. Join with sl st to 3rd ch of beg ch-4—12 dc.
Rnd 3 Ch 2 (counts as 1 sc), 1 sc in first ch-1 sp, [1 sc in next dc, 1 sc in next ch-1 sp] 11 times. Join with sl st to top of beg ch-2—24 sc.
Rnd 4 Ch 3 (counts as 1 dc), 1 dc in next 3 sc, [ch 7, 1 dc in next 4 sc] 5 times, ch 7. Join with sl st to top of beg ch-3—6 ch-7 sps.
Rnd 5 Ch 1, skip first dc, 1 sc in next dc, [(4 sc, picot, 4 sc) in next ch-7 sp, skip next 2 dc, 1 sc in next dc] 5 times, (4 sc, Picot, 4 sc) in last ch-7 sp, skip next dc. Join with sl st to first sc. Fasten off.

STITCH KEY
⭘ chain (ch)
✚ single crochet (sc)
🕈 double crochet (dc)
• slip stitch (sl st)
🝊 picot

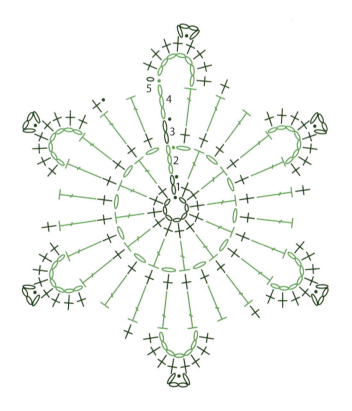

25. Wagon Wheel

STITCH GLOSSARY
CL (3-hdc Puff) [Yo and draw up a lp] 3 times in same sp, yo and draw through all 7 lps on hook.

Ch 5 and join with sl st in first ch to form ring.
Rnd 1 (RS) Ch 5 (counts as 1 tr and ch 1), [1 tr, ch 1] 11 times in ring. Join with sl st in 4th ch of beg ch-5—12 tr.
Rnd 2 [CL, ch 1] twice in first ch-1 sp, *[CL, ch 1] twice in next ch-1 sp; rep from * around. Join with sl st to top of first puff st—24 puff sts.
Rnd 3 Sl st in first ch-1 sp, ch 6 (counts as 1 tr and ch 2), 1 tr in same sp—first corner, *ch 1, 1 dc in next ch-1 sp, [ch 1, 1 hdc in next ch-1 sp] 3 times, ch 1, 1 dc in next ch-1 sp, ch 1**, (1 tr, ch 2, 1 tr) in next corner ch-1 sp; rep from * twice more, then from * to ** once. Join with sl st in 4th ch of beg ch-6. Fasten off.

STITCH KEY
- ⌒ chain (ch)
- + single crochet (sc)
- T half double crochet (hdc)
- ╪ double crochet (dc)
- ╪ treble crochet (tr)
- • slip stitch (sl st)
- ⬭ 3-half double crochet puff (CL)

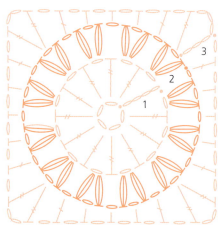

26. Daisy Puff

Ch 6 and join with sl st in first ch to form ring.
Rnd 1 (RS) Ch 5 (counts as 1 dc and ch 2), [1 dc, ch 2] 7 times in ring—8 ch-2 sps. Join with sl st in 3rd ch of beg ch-5.
Rnd 2 Ch 3 (counts as 1 dc), [4 dc in next ch-2 sp, 1 dc in dc] 7 times, 4 dc in last ch-2 sp. Join with sl st in top of beg ch-3.
Rnd 3 Sl st in next dc, ch 3 (counts as 1 dc), *1 sc in next 2 dc, 1 dc in dc, ch 5**, skip 1 dc, 1 dc in next dc; rep from * 6 times more, then from * to ** once. Join with sl st to top of beg ch-3. Fasten off.

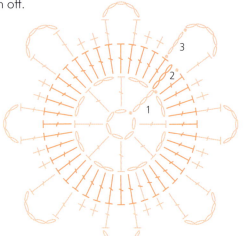

STITCH KEY
- ⌒ chain (ch)
- + single crochet (sc)
- ╪ double crochet (dc)
- • slip stitch (sl st)

27 May Flower

Ch 8 and join with sl st in first ch to form ring.
Rnd 1 (RS) Ch 1, 16 sc in ring. Skip ch 1 and join with sl st to first sc.
Rnd 2 Ch 5 (counts as 1 dc and ch 2), *skip 1 sc, 1 dc in next sc, ch 2; rep from * around, skip 1 sc. Join with sl st in 3rd ch of beg ch-5—8 ch-2 sps.
Rnd 3 Sl st in ch-2 sp, ch 1, (1 sc, 1 hdc, 1 dc, 1 hdc, 1 sc) in each ch-2 sp around. Join with sl st to first sc—8 petals.
Rnd 4 Sl st to first hdc, sl st to first dc, ch 1, sc in same st as last sl st, [ch 4, skip 4 sts, 1 sc in next dc] 7 times, ch 4. Join with sl st to first sc.
Rnd 5 Sl st in first ch-4 sp, ch 1, (1 sc, 1 hdc, 3 dc, 1 hdc, 1 sc) each ch-4 sp around. Join with sl st to first sc. Fasten off.

STITCH KEY
- chain (ch)
- single crochet (sc)
- half double crochet (hdc)
- double crochet (dc)
- slip stitch (sl st)

28. Hypericum

COLORS
A (magenta) and B (purple)

With A, ch 8 and join with sl st to form ring.
Rnd 1 Ch 1, 12 sc in ring. Skip ch 1 and join with sl st to first sc.
Rnd 2 Ch 5 (counts as 1 sc and ch 4), *skip 1 sc, 1 sc in next sc, ch 4; rep from * around. Join with sl st in 2nd ch of beg ch-5—6 ch-4 lps.
Rnd 3 In each ch-4 sp, work (1 sc, 1 hdc, 3 dc, 1 hdc, 1 sc)—6 petals. Join with sl st to first sc. Fasten off.
Rnd 4 With B and lp on hook, and working behind last rnd, *sc around post of sc on rnd 2, ch 5; rep from * around—6 ch-5 lps. Join with sl st to first sc. Fasten off.
Rnd 5 In each ch-5 sp, work (1 sc, 1 hdc, 5 dc, 1 hdc, 1 sc)—6 petals. Join with sl st to first sc. Fasten off.

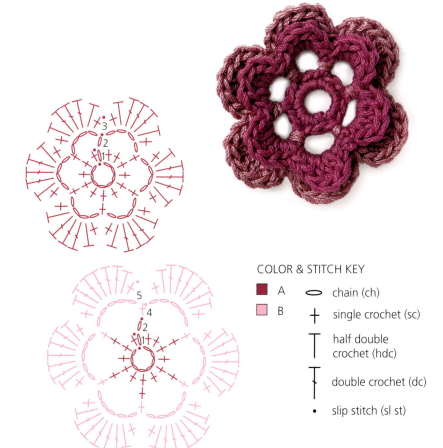

COLOR & STITCH KEY
- A
- B
- chain (ch)
- single crochet (sc)
- half double crochet (hdc)
- double crochet (dc)
- slip stitch (sl st)

29. Blazing Star

STITCH GLOSSARY

CL5 (5-tr Bobble) [Yo twice and draw up a lp, (yo and draw through 2 lps on hook) twice] 5 times in same sp or st, yo and draw through all 6 lps on hook.

CL6 (6-tr Bobble) [Yo twice and draw up a lp, (yo and draw through 2 lps on hook) twice] 6 times in same sp or st, yo and draw through all 7 lps on hook.

Ch 8 and join with sl st in first ch to form ring.
Rnd 1 (RS) Ch 7 (counts as 1 tr and ch 3), [1 tr, ch 3] 7 times in ring. Join with sl st in 4th ch of beg ch-7—8 ch-3 sps.
Rnd 2 Sl st in first ch-3 sp, ch 4, CL5 in same ch-3 sp, [ch 10, CL6 in next ch-3 sp] 7 times, ch 10. Join with sl st in top of first cluster—8 tr clusters.
Rnd 3 Ch 1, 15 sc in first ch-10 sp, *5 sc in next sp, ch 10, turn; skip 4 sc of previous sp, sl st in next sc, turn; 13 sc in ch just formed, work 10 sc more in uncompleted sp; rep from * around, end sl st across first 5 sc, ch 10, turn; skip 4 sc of previous sp, sl st in next sc, turn; 13 sc in ch just formed, sl st in base of ch-10 lp.
Rnd 4 Ch 3 (counts as 1 dc), *[skip 2 sc, 1 dc in next sc] twice, [ch 2, skip 2 sc, 1 dc in next sc] twice, ch 3, 1 dc in same sc as last dc, [ch 2, skip 2 sc, 1 dc in next sc] twice; rep from * 7 times, end [skip 2 sc, 1 dc in next sc] twice, [ch 2, skip 2 sc, 1 dc in next sc] twice, ch 3, 1 dc in same sc as last dc, ch 2, skip 2 sc, 1 dc in next sc, ch 2. Join with sl st to top of beg ch-3. Fasten off.

STITCH KEY

◯ chain (ch)

✛ single crochet (sc)

╀ double crochet (dc)

• slip stitch (sl st)

 5-treble bobble (CL5)

 6-treble bobble (CL6)

30. Grandiflora

STITCH GLOSSARY
Picot (3-ch) Ch 3, sl st in 3rd ch from hook.

Ch 7 and join with sl st in first ch to form ring.
Rnd 1 (RS) Ch 1 (counts as 1 sc throughout), 23 sc in ring. Join with sl st to beg ch-1—24 sc.
Rnd 2 Ch 1, 1 sc in each sc around. Join with sl st to beg ch-1.
Rnd 3 Ch 1, 1 sc in next sc, *Picot, 1 sc in next 2 sc; rep from * around, end last rep with Picot. Join with sl st to beg ch-1—12 Picots.
Rnd 4 Ch 8 (counts as 1 dtr and ch 4), *skip Picot, 1 dtr in next sc, ch 4; rep from * around. Join with sl st in 4th ch of beg ch-8.
Rnd 5 8 sc in each ch-4 sp around. Join with sl st to first sc.
Rnd 6 Ch 1, skip first sc, 1 sc in next 7 sc, *ch 8, skip 8 sc, 1 sc in next 8 sc; rep from * around, ch 8. Join with sl st to beg ch-1.
Rnd 7 Ch 1, skip first sc, 1 sc in next 5 sc, skip 1 sc, *15 sc in ch-8 sp, skip 1 sc, 1 sc in next 6 sc, skip 1 sc; rep from * around, end 15 sc in last ch-8 sp. Join with sl st to beg ch-1.
Rnd 8 Ch 1, skip 1 sc, 1 sc in next 3 sc, skip 1 sc, *[1 sc in next 3 sc, Picot] 4 times, 1 sc in next 3 sc, skip 1 sc, 1 sc in next 4 sc, skip 1 sc; rep from * around, end [1 sc in next 3 sc, Picot] 4 times, 1 sc in last 3 sc. Join with sl st to beg ch-1. Fasten off.

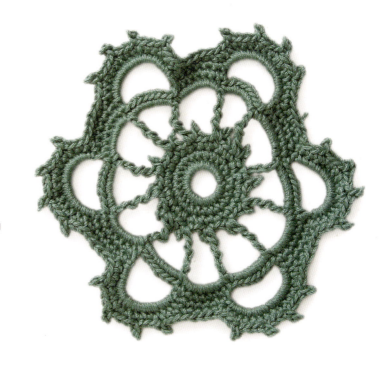

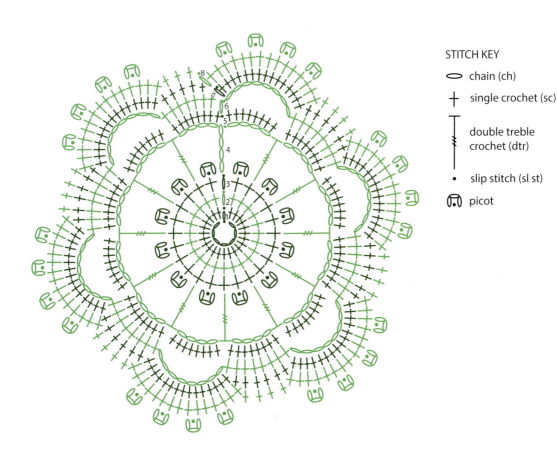

STITCH KEY
⬯ chain (ch)
✛ single crochet (sc)
╪ double treble crochet (dtr)
• slip stitch (sl st)
🝔 picot

31. Narcissus

STITCH GLOSSARY
BPdc (Back Post dc) Yo, insert hook from back to front to back around post of st directly below and draw up a lp, complete as dc.

COLORS
A (yellow), B (light pink), and C (orange)

With A, ch 5, and join with sl st to form ring.
Rnd 1 Ch 3 (counts as 1 dc and ch 1), [1 dc in ring, ch 1] 11 times. Join with sl st in 2nd ch of beg ch-3—12 ch-1 sps. Fasten off.
Rnd 2 With B and lp on hook, (1 sc, 1 hdc, 1 sc) in each ch-1 sp around. Join with sl st in top of first sc. Fasten off.
Rnd 3 With A and lp on hook, insert hook from back to front to back around post of dc from rnd 1 and make a sl st, BPdc around post of same st as sl st, ch 2, *BPdc around next dc from rnd 1, ch 2; rep from * around. Join with sl st in top of first st. Fasten off.
Rnd 4 With C, sl st in first ch-2 sp, ch 2 (counts as 1 hdc), 2 hdc in same ch-2 sp as joining, 3 hdc in each rem ch-2 sp around. Join with sl st to top of beg ch-2. Fasten off.

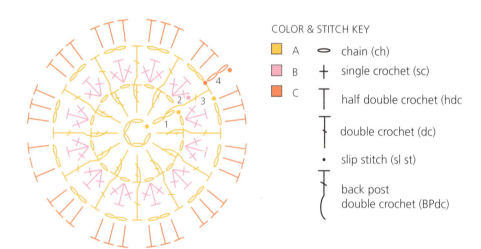

COLOR & STITCH KEY
A — chain (ch)
B — single crochet (sc)
C — half double crochet (hdc)
— double crochet (dc)
— slip stitch (sl st)
— back post double crochet (BPdc)

32. Alone Together

STITCH GLOSSARY

CL2 (2-dc Bobble) [Yo and draw up a lp, yo and draw through 2 lps on hook] twice, yo and draw through all 3 lps on hook.

CL3 (3-dc Bobble) [Yo and draw up a lp, yo and draw through 2 lps on hook] 3 times, yo and draw through all 4 lps on hook.

FIRST MOTIF

Ch 4, join with sl st to form ring.
Rnd 1 Ch 1, 8 sc in ring, join with sl st to first sc.
Rnd 2 (Ch 3, CL2) in first sc, ch 4, [CL3 in next sc, ch 4] 7 times—8 clusters. Join with sl st to top of beg CL2.
Rnd 3 Sl st in first ch-4 sp, ch 1, *(1 sc, ch 2, 1 sc, ch 4, 1 sc) in next ch-4 sp, ch 8, (1 sc, ch 4, 1 sc, ch 2, 1 sc) in next ch-4 sp; rep from * around. Join with sl st to first sc. Fasten off.

ALL REMAINING MOTIFS

Work as first motif through rnd 2.
Work rnd 3 as first motif, joining motifs in corresponding ch-8 corners or ch-4 sps as foll:

Ch-8 Corners Ch 4 on rnd 3, drop lp from hook, insert hook from front to back through corresponding ch-8 lp on first motif, pick up dropped lp of 2nd motif, ch 4, cont to work rnd 3 as established.

Ch-4 Spaces Ch 2 on rnd 3, drop lp from hook, insert hook from front to back in corresponding ch-4 lp on first motif, pick up dropped lp of 2nd motif, ch 2, cont to work rnd 3 as established.

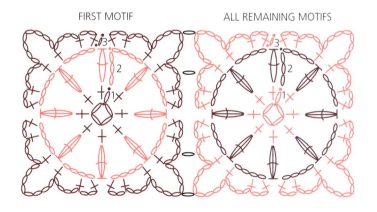

FIRST MOTIF   ALL REMAINING MOTIFS

STITCH KEY

- chain (ch)
- single crochet (sc)
- slip stitch (sl st)
- 2-double crochet cluster (CL2)
- 3-double crochet cluster (CL3)

33. Half-Star

STITCH GLOSSARY
Picot (4-ch) Ch 4, sl st in 4th ch from hook.

Ch 7 and join with sl st in first ch to form ring.
Row 1 (RS) Ch 2 (counts as 1 sc), 7 sc in ring—8 sc. Turn.
Row 2 Ch 4 (counts as 1 dc and ch 1), skip first sc, [1 dc in next sc, ch 1] 6 times, end 1 dc in top of ch-2 t-ch—7 ch-1 sps. Turn.
Row 3 Ch 1, 1 sc in first dc, sc in first ch-1 sp, [1 sc in next dc, 1 sc in next ch-1 sp] 6 times, end 1 sc in 3rd ch of ch-4 of row 3—15 sc. Turn.
Row 4 Ch 7, skip 2 sc, 1 dc in next 4 sc, [ch 7, 1 dc in next 4 sc] twice, ch 7, sl st in last sc—4 ch-7 sps. Turn.
Row 5 Ch 1, *(4 sc, Picot, 4 sc) in ch-7 sp, skip 2 dc, 1 sc in next dc, skip next dc; rep from *, end [4 sc, Picot, 4 sc] in last ch-7 sp, sl st to base of ch-7. Fasten off.

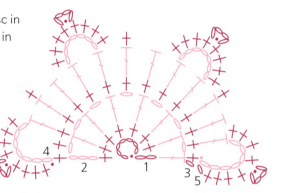

STITCH KEY
- chain (ch)
- single crochet (sc)
- double crochet (dc)
- slip stitch (sl st)
- picot

34. Flax Flower

COLORS
A (peach), B (purple), and C (light pink)

With A, ch 5 and join with sl st in first ch to form ring.
Rnd 1 (RS) Ch 3 (counts as 1 hdc and ch 1), [1 hdc in ring, ch 1] 11 times. Join with sl st in 2nd ch of beg ch-3—12 ch-1 sps. Fasten off.
Rnd 2 With B, sl st to 2nd ch of beg ch-3 of previous rnd, ch 2 (counts as 1 hdc), 1 hdc in first ch-1 sp, *ch 1, 2 hdc in next ch-1 sp; rep from * around, ch 1. Join with sl st to top of beg ch-2. Fasten off.
Rnd 3 With C and lp on hook, (1 sc, 2 hdc, 1 sc) in each ch-1 sp around. Join with sl st to first sc. Fasten off.

COLOR & STITCH KEY
- A
- B
- C
- chain (ch)
- single crochet (sc)
- half double crochet (hdc)
- slip stitch (sl st)

35. Oxalis

STITCH GLOSSARY
Spike sc Insert hook into first rnd, yo and draw up a lp in this sp to the height of the edge being worked on, yo and draw through both lps on hook.
Picot (3-ch) Ch 3, sl st in 3rd ch from hook.

COLORS
A (purple) and B (peach)

With A, ch 8 and join with sl st to form ring.
Rnd 1 Ch 1, 16 sc in ring. Join with sl st to first sc, changing to B. Fasten off A.
Rnd 2 With B, sl st in sc to join, (ch 1, 1 sc) in same st as joining, 1 sc in next sc, *(1 sc, ch 7, 1 sc) in next sc, 1 sc in next 3 sc; rep from *, end last rep 1 sc in last sc. Join with sl st to first sc.
Rnd 3 Ch 1, 1 sc in same st as joining, *skip 2 sc, (2 hdc, 15 dc, 2 hdc) into next ch-7 lp, skip 2 sc, 1 sc in next sc; rep from *, end last rep omitting 1 sc in next sc. Join with sl st to first sc. Fasten off.
Rnd 4 With A, sl st to first sc of rnd 3, Spike sc in first sc of rnd 1, *[ch 4, skip next 4 sts of rnd 3, 1 sc in next st, Picot] 3 times, ch 4, skip 4 sts**, Spike sc in next sc of rnd 1; rep from * twice more, then from * to ** once. Join with sl st to top of beg Spike sc. Fasten off.

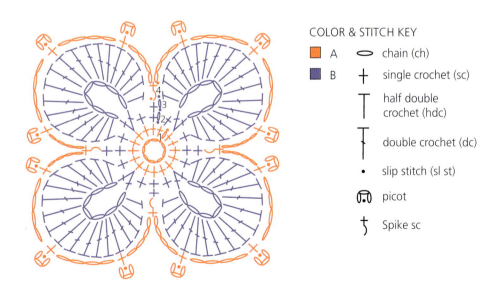

COLOR & STITCH KEY
- A — chain (ch)
- B — single crochet (sc)
- half double crochet (hdc)
- double crochet (dc)
- slip stitch (sl st)
- picot
- Spike sc

36. Skinny Stripes

COLORS
A (light green) and B (bright green)

Ch any number of sts plus 1.
Row 1 (RS) With A, 1 sc in 2nd ch from hook and in each ch across. Turn.
Rows 2–6 With A, ch 1, 1 sc in first and in each sc across. Turn. Fasten off after row 6.
Row 7 With B, ch 1, 1 sc in first and in each sc across. Fasten off. Turn.
Row 8 With A, ch 1, 1 sc in first and in each sc across. Turn.
Rep rows 2–8.

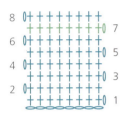

COLOR & STITCH KEY
- A chain (ch)
- B single crochet (sc)

37. Wide Stripes 1

COLORS
A (orange) and B (yellow)

Ch any number of sts plus 2.
Row 1 (RS) With A, 1 hdc in 3rd ch from hook and in each ch across. Turn.
Rows 2–5 With A, ch 2 (counts as 1 hdc throughout), skip first st, 1 hdc in next and each hdc across, end hdc in top of t-ch. Turn. Fasten off after row 5.
Rows 6–10 With B, ch 2, skip first st, 1 hdc in next and each hdc across, end hdc in top of t-ch. Turn. Fasten off after row 10.
Row 11 With A, ch 2, skip first st, 1 hdc in next and each hdc across, end hdc in top of t-ch. Turn.
Rep rows 2–11.

COLOR & STITCH KEY
- A chain (ch)
- B half double crochet (hdc)

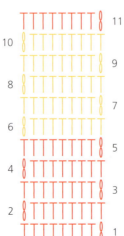

38. Wide Stripes 2

COLORS
A (orange) and B (purple)

Ch any number of sts plus 3.
Row 1 (RS) With A, 1 dc in 4th ch from hook and in each ch across. Turn.
Rows 2 and 3 With A, ch 3 (counts as 1 dc throughout), skip first st, 1 dc in next and each dc across, end dc in top of t-ch. Turn. Fasten off after row 3.
Rows 4–6 With B, ch 3, skip first st, 1 dc in next and each dc across, end dc in top of t-ch. Turn. Fasten off after row 6.
Row 7 With A, ch 3, skip first st, 1 dc in next and each dc across, end dc in top of t-ch. Turn.
Rep rows 2–7.

COLOR & STITCH KEY
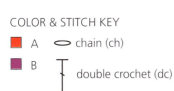
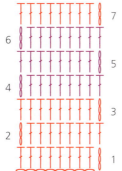

39. Striped Chevron

COLORS
A (light green), B (yellow), and C (green)

With A, ch a multiple of 10 sts plus 2.
Row 1 (RS) Work 2 sc in 2nd ch from hook, *1 sc in next 3 ch, skip 1 ch, 1 sc in next ch, skip 1 ch, 1 sc in next 3 ch, 3 sc in next ch; rep from * to last 10 ch, 1 sc in next 3 ch, skip 1 ch, 1 sc in next ch, skip 1 ch, 1 sc in next 3 ch, 2 sc in last ch. Turn.
Row 2 Ch 1, 2 sc in first sc, *1 sc in next 3 sc, skip 1 sc, 1 sc in next sc, skip 1 sc, 1 sc in next 3 sc, 3 sc in next sc; rep from * to last 10 sc, 1 sc in next 3 sc, skip 1 sc, 1 sc in next sc, skip 1 sc, 1 sc in next 3 sc, 2 sc in last sc. Fasten off. Turn.
Rows 3 and 4 With B, work row 2 twice then fasten off.
Rows 5 and 6 With C, work row 2 twice then fasten off.
Rows 7 and 8 With A, work row 2 twice then fasten off.
Rep rows 3–8.

COLOR & STITCH KEY
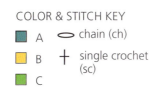

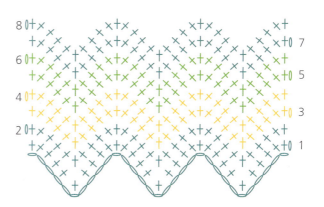

40. Three-Color Stripes

COLORS
A (orange), B (green), and C (light green)

With A, ch any number of sts plus 1.
Row 1 (RS) With A, 1 sc in 2nd ch from hook and in each ch across. Fasten off. Turn.
Row 2 With B, ch 2 (counts as 1 hdc throughout), skip first sc, 1 hdc in each sc across. Fasten off. Turn.
Row 3 With A, ch 1, 1 sc in each hdc across, end sc in top of t-ch. Fasten off. Turn.
Row 4 With C, rep row 2.
Row 5 With A, rep row 3.
Rep rows 2–5.

41. Love Camp Summer

COLORS
A (blue), B (orange), C (purple), D (green), E (light green), F (yellow), and G (white)

With A, ch any number of sts plus 2.
Row 1 (RS) With A, 1 hdc in 3rd ch from hook and in each ch across. Fasten off. Turn.
Row 2 With B, 1 sc in each st across, end sc in top of t-ch. Turn.
Rows 3 and 4 With B, 1 sc in each st across. Fasten off. Turn.
Row 5 With C, ch 3 (counts as 1 dc throughout), skip first st, 1 dc in each st across. Fasten off. Turn.
Row 6 With D, ch 2 (counts as 1 hdc throughout), skip first st, 1 hdc in each st across, end hdc in top of t-ch. Fasten off. Turn.
Row 7 With A, ch 3, skip first st, 1 dc in each st across, end dc in top of t-ch. Fasten off. Turn.
Rows 8–10 With E, rep rows 2–4.
Row 11 With F, ch 4 (counts as 1 tr throughout), skip first st, 1 tr in each st across. Fasten off. Turn.
Row 12 With D, rep row 6.
Row 13–15 With G, rep rows 2–4.
Row 16 With C, ch 2, skip first st, 1 hdc in each st across. Fasten off. Turn.
Row 17 With A, rep row 6.
Rep rows 2–17.

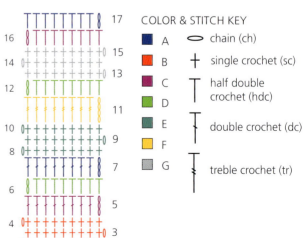

42. Scallop Stripes

COLORS
A (white), B (green), and C (purple)

With A, ch a multiple of 11 sts plus 10.
Row 1 (RS) Work 1 dc in 4th ch from hook, ch 1, skip 2 ch, 1 sc in next ch, *ch 5, skip 4 ch, 1 sc in next ch, ch 1, skip 2 ch, (1 dc, ch 1, 1 dc) in next ch, ch 1, skip 2 ch, 1 sc in next ch; rep from *, end ch 2, skip 2 ch, 1 dc in last ch. Turn.
Row 2 Ch 1, 1 sc in first dc, skip ch-2 sp, *3 dc in each of next 3 ch-1 sps, 1 sc in next ch-5 sp; rep from *, end 3 dc in last ch-1 sp, 2 dc in top of t-ch. Fasten off. Turn.
Row 3 With B, ch 4, 1 sc between 2nd and 3rd dc of first scallop, *ch 1, (1 dc, ch 1, 1 dc) in next sc, ch 1, 1 sc between first and 2nd dc of next scallop, ch 5, skip next scallop, 1 sc between 2nd and 3rd dc of next scallop; rep from *, end ch 1, 2 dc in last sc. Turn.
Row 4 With B, ch 3, 1 dc in first dc, 3 dc in ch-1 sp, *1 sc in ch-5 sp, 3 dc in each of next 3 ch-1 sps; rep from *, end 1 sc in t-ch sp. Fasten off. Turn.
Row 5 With C, ch 3, 1 dc in first sc, ch 1, *1 sc between first and 2nd dc of next scallop, ch 5, skip next scallop, 1 sc between between 2nd and 3rd dc of next scallop, ch 1, (1 dc, ch 1, 1 dc) in next sc, ch 1; rep from *, end 1 sc between first and 2nd dc of last scallop, ch 2, 1 dc in top of t-ch. Turn.
Row 6 With C, ch 1, 1 sc in first dc, skip ch-2 sp, *3 dc in each of next 3 ch-1 sps, 1 sc in next ch-5 sp; rep from *, end 3 dc in last ch-1 sp, 2 dc in top of t-ch. Fasten off. Turn.
Rows 7 and 8 With B, rep rows 3 and 4.
Rows 9 and 10 With A, rep rows 5 and 6.
Rows 11 and 12 With C, rep rows 3 and 4.
Rows 13 and 14 With A, rep rows 5 and 6.
Rep rows 3–14.

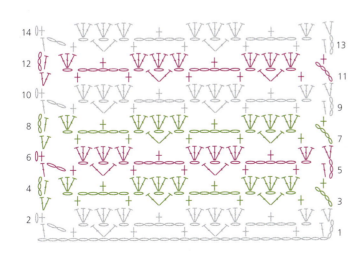

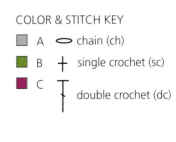

COLOR & STITCH KEY
- A — chain (ch)
- B + single crochet (sc)
- C ╀ double crochet (dc)

43. Lace Ripples

COLORS
A (yellow), B (white), C (green), and D (blue)

With A, ch a multiple of 16 sts plus 2.
Row 1 (RS) With A, 1 sc in 2nd ch from hook, *1 sc in next ch, ch 1, skip 1 ch, 1 hdc in next ch, ch 1, skip 1 ch, 1 dc in next ch, [ch 1, skip 1 ch, 1 tr in next ch] twice, ch 1, skip 1 ch, 1 dc in next ch, ch 1, skip 1 ch, 1 hdc in next ch, ch 1, skip 1 ch, 1 sc in next ch, ch 1, skip 1 ch; rep from *, end last rep 1 sc in each of last 2 ch. Fasten off. Turn.
Row 2 With B, ch 1, 1 sc in each st and ch-1 sp. Turn.
Row 3 With B, ch 1, 1 sc in each sc across. Fasten off. Turn.
Row 4 With C, ch 4 (counts as 1 tr), skip first st, *1 tr in next st, ch 1, skip 1 st, 1 dc in next st, ch 1, skip 1 st, 1 hdc in next st, [ch 1, skip 1 st, 1 sc in next st] twice, ch 1, skip 1 st, 1 hdc in next st, ch 1, skip 1 st, 1 dc in next st, ch 1, skip 1 st, 1 tr in next st, ch 1, skip 1 st; rep from *, end last rep 1 tr in each of last 2 sts. Turn.
Row 5 With C, ch 4 (counts as 1 tr), skip first st, *1 tr in next st, ch 1, skip 1 st, 1 dc in next st, ch 1, skip 1 st, 1 hdc in next st, [ch 1, skip 1 st, 1 sc in next st] twice, ch 1, skip 1 st, 1 hdc in next st, ch 1, skip 1 st, 1 dc in next st, ch 1, skip 1 st, 1 tr in next st, ch 1, skip 1 st; rep from *, end last rep 1 tr in last st, tr in top of t-ch. Fasten off. Turn.
Rows 6 and 7 With B, rep rows 2 and 3, but do not fasten off.
Rows 8 and 9 With A, ch 1, 1 sc in first st, *1 sc in next st, ch 1, skip 1 st, 1 hdc in next st, ch 1, skip 1 st, 1 dc in next st, [ch 1, skip 1 st, 1 tr in next st] twice, ch 1, skip 1 st, 1 dc in next st, ch 1, skip 1 st, 1 hdc in next st, ch 1, skip 1 st, 1 sc in next st, ch 1, skip 1 st; rep from *, end last rep 1 sc in last 2 sts. Ch 1, turn. Fasten off after row 9.
Rows 10 and 11 With B, rep rows 2 and 3.
Rows 12 and 13 With D, rep rows 4 and 5.
Rows 14 and 15 With B, rep rows 2 and 3, but do not fasten off.
Rows 16 and 17 With A, rep rows 8 and 9.
Rep rows 2–17.

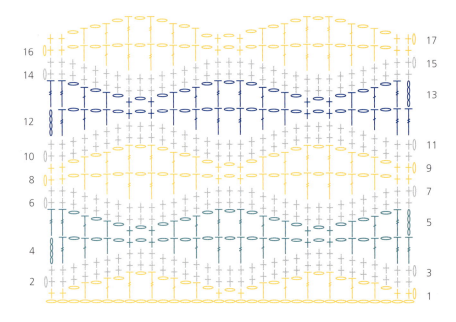

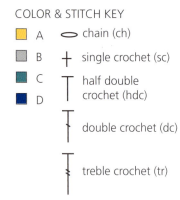

COLOR & STITCH KEY

- A — chain (ch)
- B — single crochet (sc)
- C — half double crochet (hdc)
- D — double crochet (dc)
- treble crochet (tr)

44. Diagonal Stripes

COLORS
A (magenta) and B (blue)

With A, ch a multiple of 8 sts plus 2.
Row 1 (RS) With A, 1 dc in 4th ch from hook and in next 2 ch, *with B, 1 dc in next 4 ch; with A, 1 dc in next 4 ch; rep from *, end with B, 1 dc in last 4 ch. Turn.
Row 2 With A, ch 3 (counts as 1 dc throughout), skip first st, *with B, 1 dc in next 4 sts; with A, 1 dc in next 4 sts; rep from *, end last rep with A, 1 dc in last 2 sts, 1 dc in top of t-ch. Turn.
Row 3 With A, ch 3, skip first st, 1 dc in next st, *with B, 1 dc in next 4 sts; with A, 1 dc in next 4 sts; rep from *, end last rep with A, 1 dc in last st, 1 dc in top of t-ch. Turn.
Row 4 With A, ch 3, skip first st, 1 dc in next 2 sts, *with B, 1 dc in next 4 sts; with A, 1 dc in next 4 sts; rep from *, end last rep with A, 1 dc in top of t-ch. Turn.
Row 5 With B, ch 3, skip first st, 1 dc in next 3 sts, *with A, 1 dc in next 4 sts; with B, 1 dc in next 4 sts; rep from *, end with A, 1 dc in last 3 sts, 1 dc in top of t-ch. Turn.
Row 6 With B, ch 3, skip first st, *with A, 1 dc in next 4 sts, with B, 1 dc in next 4 sts; rep from *, end last rep with B, 1 dc in last 2 sts, 1 dc in top of t-ch. Turn.
Row 7 With B, ch 3, skip first st, 1 dc in next st, *with A, 1 dc in next 4 sts; with B, 1 dc in next 4 sts; rep from *, end last rep with B, 1 dc in last st, 1 dc in top of t-ch. Turn.
Row 8 With B, ch 3, skip first st, 1 dc in next 2 sts, *with A, 1 dc in next 4 sts; with B, 1 dc in next 4 sts; rep from *, end last rep with B, 1 dc in top of t-ch. Turn.
Row 9 With A, ch 3, skip first st, 1 dc in next 3 sts, *with B, 1 dc in next 4 sts; with A, 1 dc in next 4 sts; rep from *, end with B, 1 dc in last 3 sts, 1 dc in top of t-ch. Turn.
Rep rows 2–9.

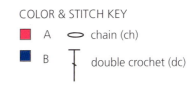

COLOR & STITCH KEY

- A
- B
- chain (ch)
- double crochet (dc)

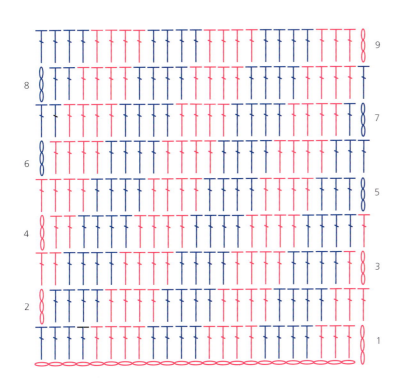

45. Twinkle, Twinkle

COLORS
A (yellow) and B (blue)

With A, ch a multiple of 8 sts plus 2.
Row 1 (RS) With B, 1 dc in 4th ch from hook and in next 5 ch, *with A, 1 dc in next 2 ch; with B, 1 dc in next 6 ch; rep from *, end with A, 1 dc in last ch. Turn.
Row 2 With A, ch 3 (counts as 1 dc throughout), skip first st, 1 dc in next 2 sts, *with B, 1 dc in next 2 sts; with A, 1 dc in next 6 sts; rep from *, end last rep with A, 1 dc in last 2 sts, 1 dc in top of t-ch. Turn.
Row 3 With A, ch 3, skip first st, *with B, 1 dc in next 6 sts; with A, 1 dc in next 2 sts; rep from *, end last rep with A, 1 dc in top of t-ch. Turn.
Row 4 With B, ch 3, skip first st, 1 dc in next 2 sts, *with A, 1 dc in next 2 sts; with B, 1 dc in next 6 sts; rep from *, end last rep with B, 1 dc in last 2 sts, 1 dc in top of t-ch. Turn.
Row 5 With B, ch 3, skip first st, *with A, 1 dc in next 6 sts; with B, 1 dc in next 2 sts; rep from *, end last rep with B, 1 dc in top of t-ch. Turn.
Row 6 With B, ch 3, skip first st, 1 dc in next 2 sts, *with A, 1 dc in next 2 sts; with B, 1 dc in next 6 sts; rep from *, end last rep with B, 1 dc in last 2 sts 1 dc in top of t-ch. Turn.
Row 7 With A, ch 3, skip first st, *with B, 1 dc in next 6 sts; with A, 1 dc in next 2 sts; rep from *, end last rep with A, 1 dc in top of t-ch. Turn.
Rep rows 2–7.

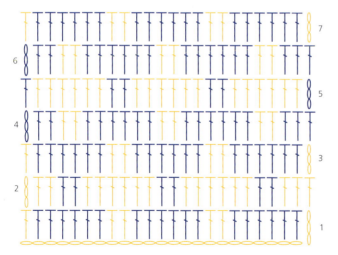

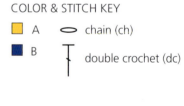

COLOR & STITCH KEY

- A — chain (ch)
- B — double crochet (dc)

46. Rainbow Chevron

STITCH GLOSSARY
Sc2tog [Insert hook in next st, yo and draw up a lp] twice, yo and draw through all 3 lps on hook.
Dc2tog [Yo, insert hook in st, yo and draw up a lp, yo, draw through 2 lps on hook] twice, yo and draw through all 3 lps on hook.

COLORS
A (white), B (berry), C (orange), D (light green), E (yellow), F (blue), and G (green)

NOTE
Work in back lps only throughout.

STRIPE SEQUENCE
Work 2 rows A, 1B, 2C, 3D, 1E, 2A, 3F, 1G.

With A, ch a multiple of 12 sts plus 3.
Row 1 (RS) Work 1 dc in 4th ch from hook, 1 dc in next 3 ch, [dc2tog over next 2 ch] twice, 1 dc in next 3 ch, 2 dc in next ch, *2 dc in next ch, 1 dc in next 3 ch, [dc2tog over next 2 ch] twice, 1 dc in next 3 ch, 2 dc in next ch; rep from * to end. Turn.
Row 2 Ch 1, 2 sc in first dc, 1 sc in next 3 dc, [sc2tog] twice, 1 sc in next 3 dc, 2 sc in next dc, *2 sc in next dc, 1 sc in next 3 dc, [sc2tog] twice, 1 sc in next 3 dc, 2 sc in next dc; rep from *, end last rep with 2 sc in top of t-ch. Turn.
Row 3 Ch 3 (counts as 1 dc), 1 dc in first sc, 1 dc in next 3 sc, [dc2tog] twice, 1 dc in next 3 sc, 2 dc in next sc, *2 dc in next sc, 1 dc in next 3 sc, [dc2tog] twice, 1 dc in next 3 sc, 2 dc in next sc; rep from * to end. Turn.
Rep rows 2 and 3, continuing stripe sequence.

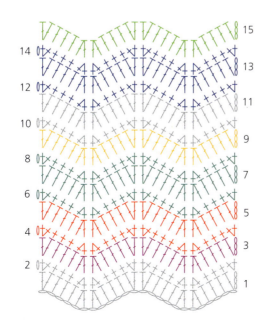

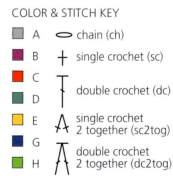

COLOR & STITCH KEY
A — chain (ch)
B — single crochet (sc)
C
D — double crochet (dc)
E
G — single crochet 2 together (sc2tog)
H — double crochet 2 together (dc2tog)

47. Safety Net

COLORS
A (blue), B (green), C (magenta), D (orange), and E (yellow)

NOTE
Work in back lps only of ch throughout pattern.

With A, ch a multiple of 4 sts.
Row 1 (RS) With A, 1 dc in 4th ch from hook, *ch 2, skip 2 ch, 1 dc in next 2 ch; rep from * across. Fasten off. Turn.
Row 2 With B, ch 4 (counts as 1 dc and ch 1 throughout), skip 1 dc, *1 dc in next 2 ch, ch 2, skip 2 dc; rep from *, end last rep 1 dc in last 2 ch, ch 1, 1 dc in top of t-ch. Fasten off. Turn.
Row 3 With C, ch 3, 1 dc in next ch, *ch 2, skip 2 dc, 1 dc in next 2 ch; rep from *, end last rep 1 dc in next ch, 1 dc in top of t-ch. Fasten off. Turn.
Row 4 With D, rep row 2.
Row 5 With E, rep row 3.
Row 6 With B, rep row 2.
Row 7 With C, rep row 3.
Row 8 With A, rep row 2.
Rep rows 2–8.

48. Jagged Stripes

COLORS
A (orange) and B (blue)

NOTE
You may either fasten off when changing colors or carry the unused color up the side the work, taking care to keep an even tension so the right-hand edge does not pull in.

With A, ch a multiple of 2 sts.
Row 1 (RS) With A, 1 sc in 2nd ch from hook, *ch 1, skip 1 ch, 1 sc in next ch; rep from * to end. Turn.
Row 2 With A, ch 1, 1 sc in first sc, *1 sc in next ch-1 sp, ch 1, skip 1 sc; rep from *, end 1 sc in last ch-1 sp, 1 sc in last sc. Turn.
Row 3 With B, ch 1, 1 sc in first sc, *ch 1, skip next sc, 1 sc in next ch-1 sp; rep from *, end ch 1, skip next sc, 1 sc in last sc. Turn.
Row 4 With B, ch 1, 1 sc in first sc, *1 sc in next ch-1 sp, ch 1, skip 1 sc; rep from *, end 1 sc in last ch-1 sp, 1 sc in last sc. Turn.
Rows 5 and 6 With A, rep rows 3 and 4.
Rep rows 3–6.

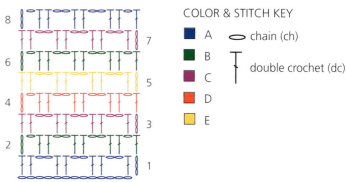

49. We Are Three

STITCH GLOSSARY
CL (3-tr Bobble) [Yo twice and draw up a lp, (yo and draw through 2 lps on hook) twice] 3 times in same ch or bottom lp, yo and draw through all 4 lps on hook.

NOTE
Pattern is worked first on one side of foundation ch, then repeated on opposite side of foundation ch to complete floral strip.

Ch a multiple of 8 sts plus 5.
FIRST SIDE
Row 1 (RS) 1 dc in 4th ch from hook, *skip 3 ch, [(CL, ch 3) twice, CL] in next ch, skip 3 ch, 1 dc in next ch; rep from * end 1 dc in last ch. Turn.
Row 2 Ch 3 (counts as 1 dc), skip first dc, 1 dc in next dc, *ch 3, 1 sc in next ch-3 sp, ch 3, 1 dc in next ch-3 sp, 1 dc in dc; rep from * end 1 dc in top of t-ch. Fasten off.

SECOND SIDE
Rotate work 180 degrees to begin working in bottom lps of foundation ch. Join yarn in first lp.
Row 1 (RS) Ch 3, 1 dc in next bottom lp, *skip 3 lps, [(CL, ch 3) twice, CL] in next lp, skip 3 lps, 1 dc in next lp; rep from * end 1 dc in last lp. Turn.
Row 2 Ch 3 (counts as 1 dc), skip first dc, 1 dc in next dc, *ch 3, 1 sc in next ch-3 sp, ch 3, 1 dc in next ch-3 sp, 1 dc in next dc; rep from * end 1 dc in top of t-ch. Fasten off.

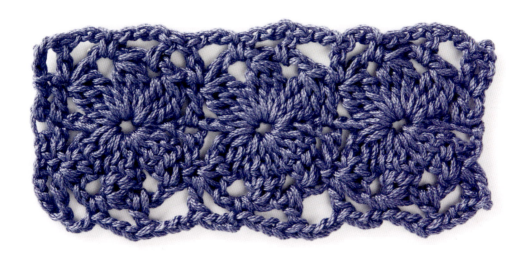

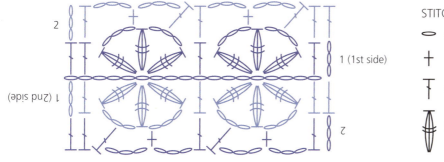

STITCH KEY
- chain (ch)
- single crochet (sc)
- double crochet (dc)
- 3-treble crochet bobble (CL)

50. Chevron Mesh

STITCH GLOSSARY

Dc2tog [Skip next ch, yo, insert hook into next ch, yo, draw up a lp, yo and draw through 2 lps on hook] twice, yo and draw through all 3 lps on hook.

Dc3tog [Yo, insert hook in next st, yo and draw up a lp, yo, draw through 2 lps on hook] 3 times, yo and draw through all 4 lps on hook.

Ch 30 sts.
Row 1 (RS) Work 1 dc in 5th ch from hook, [ch 1, skip 1 ch, 1 dc in next ch] 5 times, ch 1, skip 1 ch, ([1 dc, ch 1] twice, 1 dc) in next ch, [ch 1, skip 1 ch, 1 dc in next ch] 5 times, ch 1, skip 1 ch, dc2tog. Turn.
Row 2 Ch 2 (counts as 1 dc), skip first dec, 1 dc in next dc, [ch 1, 1 dc in next dc] 5 times, ([ch 1, 1 dc] 3 times) in next dc, [ch 1, 1 dc in next dc] 6 times, dc3tog. Turn.
Row 3 Ch 2 (counts as 1 dc), skip first dec, 1 dc in next dc, [ch 1, 1 dc in next dc] 6 times, ([ch 1, 1 dc] 3 times) in next dc, [ch 1, 1 dc in next dc] 5 times, ch 1, dc3tog. Turn.
Rep rows 2 and 3.

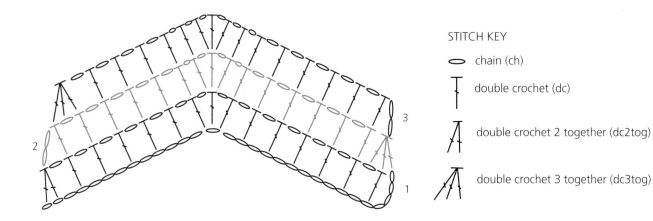

STITCH KEY

◯— chain (ch)

┬ double crochet (dc)

⋀ double crochet 2 together (dc2tog)

⋀ double crochet 3 together (dc3tog)

51. Fanfare

Ch a multiple of 6 sts plus 4.
Row 1 (RS) Work 1 sc in 2nd ch from hook, 1 sc in next 2 ch, *ch 3, skip 3 ch, 1 sc in next 3 ch; rep from * across. Turn.
Row 2 Ch 1, 1 sc in first 2 sc, *skip 1 sc, 5 dc in ch-3 sp, skip 1 sc, 1 sc in next sc; rep from *, end 1 sc in last sc. Turn.
Row 3 Ch 4 (counts as 1 sc and ch 3), skip (2 sc, 1 dc), 1 sc in next 3 dc, *ch 3, skip (1 dc, 1 sc, 1 dc), 1 sc in next 3 dc; rep from *, end ch 3, skip (1 dc, 1 sc), 1 sc in last sc. Turn.
Row 4 Ch 3 (counts as 1 dc), 3 dc in first ch-3 sp, *skip 1 sc, 1 sc in next sc, skip 1 sc, 5 dc in ch-3 sp; rep from *, end last rep 4 dc in last ch-3 sp. Turn.
Row 5 Ch 1, 1 sc in first 3 dc, *ch 3, skip (1 dc, 1 sc, 1 dc), 1 sc in next 3 dc; rep from * across. Turn.
Rep rows 2–5.

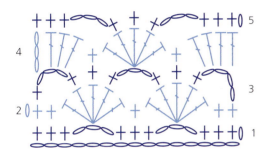

STITCH KEY
⌒ chain (ch)
+ single crochet (sc)
⊤ double crochet (dc)

52. Shell and Bar

STITCH GLOSSARY
Shell (2 dc, ch 1, 2 dc) in same ch.

Ch a multiple of 15 sts plus 7.
Row 1 (RS) Work 1 dc in 4th ch from hook, 1 dc in next 3 ch, *skip 2 ch, shell in next ch, skip 4 ch, shell in next ch, skip 2 ch, 1 dc in next 5 ch; rep from * to end. Turn.
Row 2 Ch 3 (counts as 1 dc), skip first dc, 1 dc in next 4 dc, *[shell in ch-1 sp of shell] twice, 1 dc in next 5 dc; rep from *, end last rep 1 dc in last 4 dc, 1 dc in top of t-ch. Turn.
Rep row 2.

STITCH KEY
⌒ chain (ch)
⊤ double crochet (dc)

53. Solomon's Knot

STITCH GLOSSARY
SK (Solomon's Knot) Lengthen lp as required, *yo and draw through lp on hook, keeping the single back strand of long chain separate from the 2 front strands, insert hook under single back thread, yo and draw lp through, yo and draw through both lps.*
ESK (Edge Solomon's Knot) These form the base "chain" and edges. Lengthen lp two-thirds the length of MSK's (approx 1"/2.5cm long) and work as for SK.
MSK (Main Solomon's Knot) These form the main fabric. Lengthen lp one and one-half times as long as ESK's (approx 1¼"/3cm long) and work as for SK.

Base chain Ch 2. 1 Sc in 2nd ch from hook, 4 ESK, 1 MSK.
Row 1 Skip 3 lps from hook, 1 sc in sc, 2 MSK, skip 4 lps from hook, 1 sc in last sc (first sc of base chain). Turn.
Row 2 3 MSK, skip 4 lps from hook , 1 sc in sc (1st 4-lp diamond), 2 MSK, skip 4 lps from hook, 1 sc in sc (2nd 4-lp diamond). Turn.
Row 3 3 MSK, skip 4 lps from hook, 1 sc in sc, *2 MSK, skip 4 lps from hook, 1 sc in sc*, 2 MSK, slip 3 lps from hook, (insert hook in next sc, yo and draw up lp, lengthening to approx 1¼"/3cm, yo and draw through long lp only, keeping the single back strand of this long st separate from the 2 front strands, insert hook under this single back strand, yo and draw up lp, yo and draw through 3 lps) (three 4-lp diamonds).

Row 4 Rep row 3, adding one 4-lp diamond on each row by rep between *'s.
Row 5 2 MSK, skip 3 lps from hook, 1 sc in sc, *1 MSK, skip 2 lps, 1 sc in next sc; rep from *, end 2 MSK, skip 3 lps from hook, 1 sc in sc along side. Fasten off.

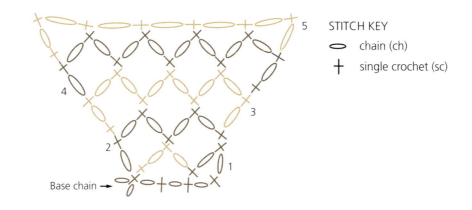

STITCH KEY
○ chain (ch)
+ single crochet (sc)

54. Mesh Stitch

Ch a multiple of 3 sts plus 8.
Row 1 (RS) Work 1 dc in back lp of 8th ch from hook, *ch 2, skip 2 ch, 1 dc in back lp of next ch; rep from *, end 1 dc in back lp of last ch. Turn.
Row 2 Ch 5 (counts as 1 dc and ch 2), skip first dc and 2 ch, *1 dc in back lp of next dc, ch 2, skip 2 ch; rep from *, end 1 dc in 3rd ch of t-ch of row below. Turn.
Rep row 2.

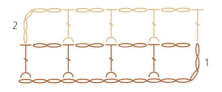

STITCH KEY
- chain (ch)
- double crochet (dc)
- double crochet in back loop only (dc in back lp)

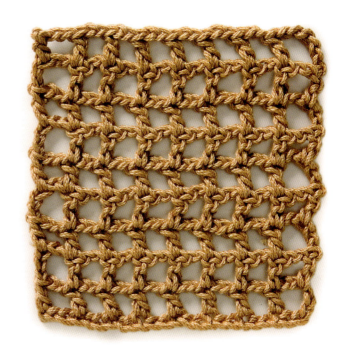

55. Stacked Clusters

STITCH GLOSSARY
CL [Yo, insert hook in next dc, yo and draw up lp, yo and draw through 2 lps on hook] 5 times, yo and draw through all 6 lps on hook.

Ch a multiple of 6 sts plus 3.
Row 1 (RS) 5 dc in 6th ch from hook, skip 2 ch, 1 dc in next ch, *skip 2 ch, 5 dc in next ch, skip 2 ch, 1 dc in next ch; rep from * to end. Turn.
Row 2 Ch 5, skip first dc, *CL over next 5 dc, ch 2, 1 dc in next dc, ch 2; rep from *, end CL over last 5 dc, ch 2, 1 dc in top of t-ch. Turn.
Row 3 Ch 3, skip 2 ch, 5 dc in CL, *skip 2 ch, 1 dc in next dc, skip 2 ch, 5 dc in next CL; rep from *, end skip 2 ch, 1 dc in 3rd ch of t-ch. Turn.
Rep rows 2 and 3.

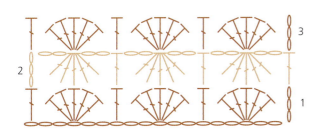

STITCH KEY
- chain (ch)
- double crochet (dc)

56. Filet

Ch a multiple of 2 sts plus 6.
Row 1 (RS) Work 1 dc in 6th ch from hook, *ch 1, skip 1 ch, 1 dc in next ch; rep from * to end. Turn.
Row 2 Ch 4 (counts as 1 dc and ch 1), skip first dc and 1 ch, *1 dc in next dc, ch 1, skip 1 ch; rep from *, end 1 dc in 2nd ch of t-ch of row below. Turn.
Rep row 2.

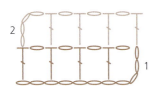

STITCH KEY
- chain (ch)
- double crochet (dc)

57. Picot

Ch a multiple of 7 sts plus 2.
Row 1 (RS) Work 1 sc in 4th ch from hook, *ch 3, 1 sc in same ch as last sc, 1 sc in next ch, ch 2, skip 2 ch, 1 sc in next ch; rep from * to end. Turn.
Rows 2 and 3 Ch 3, *1 dc in next ch-2 sp, ch 3, 1 sc in top of last dc, 1 dc in same sp as last dc, ch 2; rep from *, end 1 dc in t-ch. Turn.
Rep rows 2 and 3.

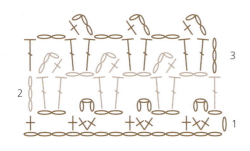

STITCH KEY
- chain (ch)
- single crochet (sc)
- double crochet (dc)

58. Shell Pattern 1

STITCH GLOSSARY
Shell (2 dc, ch 1, 2 dc) in same st.

Ch a multiple of 4 sts.
Row 1 (RS) Shell in 4th ch from hook, *skip 3 ch, shell in next ch; rep from * to end. Turn.
Row 2 Ch 3, *shell in ch-1 sp of next shell; rep from * to end. Turn.
Rep row 2.

STITCH KEY
chain (ch)
double crochet (dc)

59. Petal Mesh

STITCH GLOSSARY
Petal [Yo, insert hook into 4th ch from hook, yo and draw up a lp, yo and draw through 2 lps on hook] twice, [yo and draw through 2 lps on hook] twice.

(make odd number of petals by working row 1)
Row 1 Ch 5, make petal, *ch 4, make petal; rep from * for desired odd number of petals. Turn.
Row 2 Ch 7, petal in 4th ch from hook, *1 sc between first and 2nd petals of row 1, ch 4, make petal; rep from *, end 1 dc in first ch of row 1. Turn.
Row 3 Ch 7, petal in 4th ch from hook, *ch 4, make petal, skip 2 petals, 1 sc in sc, ch 4, make petal; rep from *, end ch 4, make petal, 1 dc in ch-sp. Turn.
Row 4 Ch 7, Petal in 4th ch from hook, *ch 4, make petal, skip 2 petals, 1 sc in between 3rd and 4th petals of previous row, ch 4, make petal; rep from *, end 1 dc in ch-sp. Turn.
Rep row 4.

STITCH KEY
chain (ch)
single crochet (sc)
double crochet (dc)
petal

60. Starburst Square

Ch 17 sts.

Row 1 (RS) Skip first 3 ch from hook (counts as 1 dc), 1 dc in next ch and in each ch to end—15 dc. Turn.

Row 2 Ch 3 (counts as 1 dc throughout), skip first dc, 1 dc in next dc, ch 5, [skip 2 dc, 1 tr in next dc] 3 times, ch 5, skip 2 dc, 1 dc in last dc, 1 dc in top of t-ch. Turn.

Row 3 Ch 3, skip first dc, 1 dc in next dc, ch 4, skip 4 ch, 1 sc in next ch, 1 sc in next 3 tr, 1 sc in next ch, ch 4, skip 4 ch, 1 dc in last dc, 1 dc in top of t-ch. Turn.

Row 4 Ch 3, skip first dc, 1 dc in next dc, ch 5, skip (ch-4 sp, 1 sc), 1 sc in next 3 sc, ch 5, skip (1 sc, ch-4 sp), 1 dc in last dc, 1 dc in top of t-ch. Turn.

Row 5 Ch 3, skip first dc, 1 dc in next dc, ch 2, skip ch-5 sp, [1 tr in next sc, ch 2] 3 times, skip ch-5 sp, 1 dc in last dc, 1 dc in top of t-ch. Turn.

Row 6 Ch 3, skip first dc, 1 dc in each st and ch across, end 1 dc in top of t-ch. Turn.

Row 7 Ch 3, skip first dc, 1 dc in each dc across, end 1 dc in top of t-ch. Turn.

Rep rows 2–7.

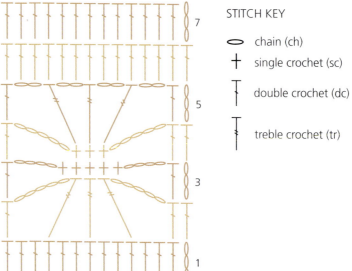

STITCH KEY

◯ chain (ch)

✝ single crochet (sc)

⊤ double crochet (dc)

⊤ treble crochet (tr)

61. Gilded Fans

Ch a multiple of 8 sts plus 5.

Row 1 (RS) Work 1 dc in 4th ch from hook, *ch 3, skip 2 ch, 1 sc in next 3 ch, ch 3, skip 2 ch, (1 dc, ch 3, 1 dc) in next ch; rep from *, end last rep ch 3, skip 2 ch, 1 dc in last 2 ch. Turn.

Row 2 Ch 3 (counts as 1 dc), 3 dc in sp between 1st and 2nd dc of row below, *ch 3, 1 sc in 2nd sc of 3-sc group, ch 3, skip next ch-3 sp, 7 dc in next ch-3 sp; rep from *, end ch 3, 1 sc in 2nd sc of last 3-sc group, ch 3, skip last ch-3 sp, 4 dc in sp between last dc and t-ch sp. Turn.

Row 3 Ch 1, 1 sc in next 4 dc, *ch 5, skip next 2 ch-3 sps, 1 sc in next 7 dc; rep from *, end ch 5, skip next 2 ch-3 sps, 1 sc in last 3 dc, 1 sc in top of t-ch. Turn.

Row 4 Ch 1, 1 sc in first sc, *ch 3, (1 dc, ch 3, 1 dc) in 3rd ch of next ch-5 sp, ch 3, skip 2 sc of next 7-sc group, 1 sc in next 3 sc; rep from *, end ch 3, (1 dc, ch 3, 1 dc) in 3rd ch of last ch-5 sp, ch 3, skip 2 sc of last 4-sc group, 1 sc in last sc. Turn.

Row 5 Ch 4, skip 1st ch-3 sp, 7 dc in ch-3 sp between dc, *ch 3, 1 sc in 2nd sc of 3-sc group, ch 3, skip next ch-sp, 7 dc in next ch sp between dc; rep from *, end ch 3, skip last ch-sp, 1 sc in last sc. Turn.

Row 6 Ch 3, *1 sc in next 7 dc, ch 5; rep from *, end last rep ch 2, 1 sc in first ch of beg ch-4 of row below. Turn.

Row 7 Ch 5 (counts as 1 dc and t-ch), 1 dc in first sc, *ch 3, skip 2 sc, 1 sc in next 3 sc, ch 3, (1 dc, ch 3, 1 dc) in 3rd ch of next ch-5 sp; rep from *, end ch 3, skip 2 sc, 1 sc in next 3 sc, ch 3, (1 dc, ch 3, 1 dc) in 1st ch of t-ch of row below. Turn.

Rep rows 2–7, end with row 3 or 6.

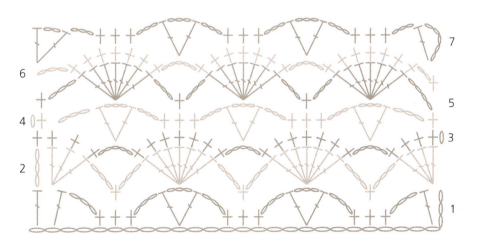

STITCH KEY
- chain (ch)
- single crochet (sc)
- double crochet (dc)

62. Gilded Arches

STITCH GLOSSARY
MP (make picot) (1 sc, ch 3, 1 sc) in same st.

Ch a multiple of 7 sts plus 4.
Row 1 (RS) Work 1 hdc in 3rd ch from hook, 1 hdc in next ch, *ch 3, skip 2 ch, 1 sc in next ch, ch 3, skip 2 ch, 1 hdc in next 2 ch; rep from * to end. Turn.
Row 2 Ch 2, 1 hdc in first 2 hdc, *ch 3, MP in next sc, ch 3, 1 hdc in next 2 hdc; rep from * to end. Turn.
Row 3 Ch 1, 1 sc in first 2 hdc, *1 sc in next ch-3 sp, ch 5, skip picot, 1 sc in next ch-3 sp, 1 sc in next 2 hdc; rep from * to end. Turn.
Row 4 Ch 1, 1 sc in first 2 sc, *skip 1 sc, 7 sc in ch-5 sp, skip 1 sc, 1 sc in next 2 sc; rep from * to end. Turn.
Row 5 Ch 2, 1 hdc in first 2 sc, *ch 3, skip 3 sc, 1 sc in next sc, ch 3, skip 3 sc, 1 hdc in next 2 sc; rep from * to end. Turn.
Rep rows 2–5.

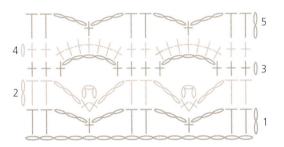

STITCH KEY
◯ chain (ch)
+ single crochet (sc)
T half double crochet (hdc)
 make picot (MP)

63. Barleycorn

STITCH GLOSSARY
Full scallop ([Ch 1, 1 dc] twice, ch 1) in next st.
Beg half scallop (1 dc, ch 1) in first sc.
End half scallop (Ch 1, 2 dc) in last sc.

Ch a multiple of 6 sts plus 2.
Row 1 (RS) Work 1 sc in 2nd ch from hook, *skip 2 ch, full scallop in next ch, skip 2 ch, 1 sc in next ch; rep from * to end. Turn.
Row 2 Ch 3 (counts as 1 dc), beg half scallop, *1 sc in center ch-1 sp of next scallop, full scallop in next sc; rep from *, end half scallop. Turn.
Row 3 Ch 1, 1 sc in first dc, *full scallop in next sc, 1 sc in center ch-1 sp of next scallop; rep from *, end last rep full scallop in last sc, 1 sc in top of t-ch. Turn.
Rep rows 2 and 3.

STITCH KEY
◯ chain (ch)
+ single crochet (sc)
T double crochet (dc)

64. Victory

STITCH GLOSSARY
V-st (Yo and draw up lp, yo and draw through 2 lps on hook) in first st, skip 1 st (or 3 ch), (yo and draw up lp, yo and draw through 2 lps) in next st (or ch), yo and draw through all 3 lps on hook.

Ch a multiple of 3 sts.
Row 1 (RS) Beg V-st in 4th ch from hook, *ch 3, V-st in last ch of previous V-st; rep from * to end. Turn.
Row 2 Ch 3, V-st in first V-st, *ch 3, V-st in last st of previous V-st; rep from * end last rep with ch 3, V-st in last st of previous V-st and in top of t-ch. Turn.
Rep row 2.

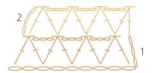

STITCH KEY
— chain (ch)
⋀ V-st

65. Star Mesh

Ch a multiple of 4 sts plus 3.
Row 1 (RS) Yo twice, insert hook in 5th ch from hook and draw up lp, *yo and draw through 2 lps (3 lps on hook and first leg of CrTr), yo, skip 1 ch, insert hook in next ch and draw up a lp, [yo and draw through 2 lps on hook] 4 times (1 lp on hook and 2nd leg of CrTr), ch 1, yo, insert hook in middle of CrTr where legs meet and draw up lp, [yo and draw through 2 lps on hook] twice—CrTr completed, ch 1, skip 1 ch, yo twice, insert hook in next ch and draw up lp; rep from *, end CrTr in last 3 ch. Turn.
Rows 2 and 3 Ch 4, skip first st and ch-1 sp, *CrTr over 2nd leg of CrTr and first leg of next CrTr of previous row, ch 1; rep from *, end CrTr over 2nd leg of CrTr and top of ch-4 t-ch of previous row. Turn.
Rep rows 2 and 3.

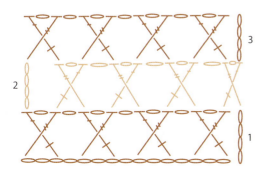
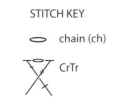

STITCH KEY
— chain (ch)
✕ CrTr

66. Tipsy Triangles

Ch a multiple of 10 sts plus 3.
Set-up row (WS) 1 sc in 2nd ch from hook and in each ch to end. Turn.
Row 1 (RS) Ch 3 (counts as 1 dc throughout), skip first sc, 1 dc in next sc, *ch 4, skip 4 sc, 1 sc in next sc, ch 4, skip 4 sc, 3 dc in next sc; rep from *, end last rep ch 4, skip 4 sc, 1 dc in last 2 sc. Turn.
Row 2 Ch 3, skip first dc, *2 dc in next dc, ch 3, skip ch-4 sp, 1 sc in next sc, ch 3, skip ch-4 sp, 2 dc in next dc, 1 dc in next dc; rep from *, end last rep 1 dc in top of t-ch. Turn.
Row 3 Ch 3, skip first dc, 1 dc in next dc, *2 dc in next dc, ch 2, skip ch-3 sp, 1 dc in sc, ch 2, skip ch-3 sp, 2 dc in next dc, 1 dc in next 3 dc; rep from *, end last rep 1 dc in last dc, 1 dc in top of t-ch. Turn.
Row 4 Ch 3, skip first dc, 1 dc in next 2 dc, 2 dc in next dc, *ch 1, skip (ch-2 sp, 1 dc, ch-2 sp), 2 dc in next dc, 1 dc in next 5 dc, 2 dc in next dc; rep from * across, end last rep 1 dc in last 2 dc, 1 dc in top of t-ch. Turn.
Row 5 Ch 1, 1 sc in first dc, *ch 4, skip next 4 dc, 3 dc in ch-1 sp, ch 4, skip next 4 dc, 1 sc in next dc; rep from *, end last rep 1 sc in top of t-ch. Turn.
Row 6 Ch 1, 1 sc in first sc, *ch 3, skip ch-4 sp, 2 dc in next dc, 1 dc in dc, 2 dc in next dc, ch 3, skip ch-4 sp, 1 sc in sc; rep from * to end. Turn.
Row 7 Ch 5 (counts as 1 dc and ch 2), *skip ch-3 sp, 2 dc in next dc, 1 dc in next 3 dc, 2 dc in next dc, ch 2, skip ch-3 sp, 1 dc in sc, ch 2; rep from *, end last rep 1 dc in last sc. Turn.
Row 8 Ch 3, skip first dc, *skip ch-2 sp, 2 dc in next dc, 1 dc in next 5 dc, 2 dc in next dc, ch 1, skip (ch-2 sp, 1 dc); rep from *, end skip ch-2 sp, 2 dc in next dc, 1 dc in next 5 dc, 2 dc in last dc, 1 dc in 3rd ch of ch-5 t-ch. Turn.
Row 9 Ch 3, 1 dc in first dc, *ch 4, skip 4 dc, 1 sc in next dc, ch 4, skip 4 dc, 3 dc in ch-1 sp; rep from *, end last rep 2 dc in top of t-ch. Turn.
Rep rows 2–9.

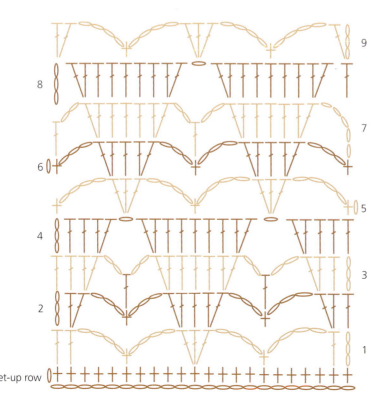

STITCH KEY

◯ chain (ch)

✛ single crochet (sc)

╈ double crochet (dc)

67. Reversible Mesh

Ch a multiple of 2 sts plus 4.
Row 1 (RS) Work 1 dc in 4th ch from hook, *ch 1, skip 1 ch, 1 dc in next ch; rep from * to end. Turn.
Row 2 Ch 3, 1 dc in first ch-1 sp, *ch 1, 1 dc in next ch-1 sp; rep from *, end ch 1, 1 dc in top of t-ch of row below. Turn.
Rep row 2.

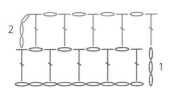

STITCH KEY
◯ chain (ch)
𝍿 double crochet (dc)

68. Network

Ch a multiple of 8 sts plus 5.
Row 1 (RS) Work 1 dc in 4th ch from hook, 1 dc in next ch, *skip 2 ch, 5 dc in next ch, skip 2 ch, 1 dc in next 3 ch; rep from * to end. Turn.
Row 2 Ch 3 (counts as 1 dc throughout), skip first dc, 1 dc in next 2 dc, *skip 2 dc, 5 dc in next dc, skip 2 dc, 1 dc in next 3 dc; rep from *, end last rep 1 dc in next 2 dc, 1 dc in top of t-ch. Turn.
Row 3 Ch 3, skip first dc, 1 dc in next 2 sts, *2 dc in sp between 3 dc and 5-dc group, ch 3, 2 dc in sp between 5-dc group and 3 dc, 1 dc in next 3 sts; rep from * to end. Turn.
Row 4 Ch 3, skip first dc, 1 dc in next 2 dc, *skip 2 dc, 5 dc in ch-3 sp, skip 2 dc, 1 dc in next 3 dc; rep from *, end last rep 1 dc in next 2 dc, 1 dc in top of t-ch. Turn.
Rep rows 3 and 4.

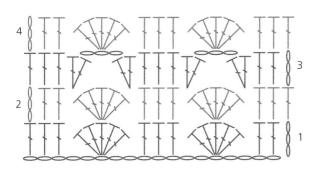

STITCH KEY
◯ chain (ch)
𝍿 double crochet (dc)

69. Long Loop Mesh

STITCH GLOSSARY
Long dc Yo, insert hook in next ch, yo and draw up a ¾"/2cm long lp, [yo and draw through 2 lps on hook] twice.

Ch a multiple of 2 sts.
Row 1 (RS) Long dc in 6th ch from hook, *ch 1, skip 1 ch, long dc in next ch; rep from * to end. Turn.
Rows 2 and 3 Ch 4 (counts as 1 long dc and ch 1 throughout), skip first ch-1 sp, *long dc in next long dc, ch 1, skip next ch-1 sp; rep from *, end long dc in 3rd ch of ch-4 t-ch. Turn.
Rep rows 2 and 3.

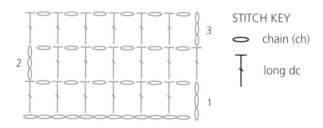

STITCH KEY
◯ chain (ch)
┼ long dc

70. Berry Clusters

Ch a multiple of 3 sts plus 4.
Row 1 (RS) Work 1 dc in 5th ch from hook, (ch 1, 1 dc) in same ch, *skip 2 ch, (1 dc, ch 1, 1 dc) in next ch; rep from *, end skip 1 ch, 1 dc in last ch. Turn.
Rows 2 and 3 Ch 3, skip first dc, *(1 dc, ch 1, 1 dc) in next ch-1 sp; rep from *, end 1 dc in top of t-ch. Turn.
Rep rows 2 and 3.

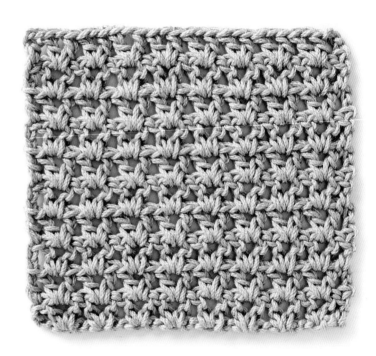

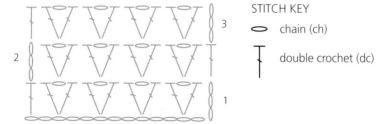

STITCH KEY
◯ chain (ch)
┬ double crochet (dc)

71. Colosseum

Ch a multiple of 12 sts plus 4.
Row 1 (RS) Work 1 dc in 4th ch from hook and in each ch to end. Turn.
Row 2 Ch 3 (counts as 1 dc throughout), skip first dc, 1 dc in next 2 dc, *ch 2, skip 2 dc, 1 dc in next 4 dc, rep from *, end last rep 1 dc in next 2 dc, 1 dc in top of t-ch. Turn.
Row 3 Ch 3, skip first dc, 1 dc in next 2 dc, *2 dc in ch-2 sp, 1 dc in next dc, ch 2, skip 2 dc, 1 dc in next dc; rep from *, end 2 dc in last ch-2 sp, 1 dc in next 2 dc, 1 dc in top of t-ch. Turn.
Row 4 Ch 3, skip first dc, 1 dc in next dc, *ch 2, skip 2 dc, 1 dc in next 2 dc, ch 2, skip ch-2 sp, 1 dc in next 2 dc, ch 2, skip 2 dc, 2 dc in ch-2 sp; rep from *, end last rep 1 dc in last dc, 1 dc in top of t-ch. Turn.
Row 5 Ch 3, skip first dc, 1 dc in next dc, *ch 2, skip ch-2 sp, 1 dc in next 2 dc; rep from *, end last rep 1 dc in last dc, 1 dc in t-ch. Turn.
Row 6 Ch 3, skip first dc, 1 dc in next dc, *2 dc in ch-2 sp, 1 dc in next 2 dc; rep from *, end last rep 1 dc in last dc, 1 dc in top of t-ch. Turn.
Rep rows 2–6.

STITCH KEY
- chain (ch)
- double crochet (dc)

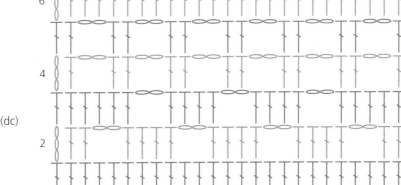

72. Fishnet Chains

Ch a multiple of 4 sts plus 1.
Row 1 (RS) Sl st in 5th ch from hook, *ch 5, skip 3 ch, sl st in next ch; rep from * to end. Turn.
Rows 2 and 3 Ch 4, sl st in 3rd ch of first ch-5 lp, *ch 5, sl st into next ch-5 lp; rep from *, end ch 5, sl st in 3rd ch of ch-4 t-ch. Turn.
Rep rows 2 and 3.

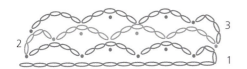

STITCH KEY
- chain (ch)
- slip stitch (sl st)

73. Checkerboard

Ch a multiple of 6 sts plus 5.
Row 1 (RS) Work 1 sc in 2nd ch from hook and in each ch across. Turn.
Row 2 Ch 3 (counts as 1 dc throughout), skip first sc, 1 dc in next 3 sc, *ch 2, skip next 2 sc, 1 dc in next 4 sc; rep from * to end. Turn.
Row 3 Ch 5 (counts as 1 dc and ch 2), skip first dc, *skip next 2 dc, 1 dc in next dc, 2 dc in ch-2 sp, 1 dc in next dc, ch 2; rep from *, end skip last 2 dc, 1 dc in top of t-ch. Turn.
Row 4 Ch 3, *2 dc in ch-2 sp, 1 dc in next dc, ch 2, skip 2 dc, 1 dc in next dc; rep from *, end 2 dc in last ch-2 sp, 1 dc in 3rd ch of ch-5 t-ch. Turn.
Rows 5 and 6 Rep rows 3 and 4.
Row 7 Ch 1, 1 sc in each dc and 2 sc in each ch-2 sp across, end 1 sc in top of t-ch. Turn.
Row 8 Ch 1, 1 sc in each sc across.
Rep rows 2–8.

STITCH KEY
- ○ chain (ch)
- + single crochet (sc)
- ╪ double crochet (dc)

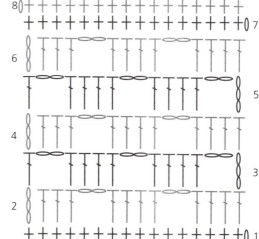

74. Shell Pattern 2

STITCH GLOSSARY
Shell ([1 dc, ch 1] 3 times, 1 dc) in same st.

Ch a multiple of 5 sts plus 4.
Row 1 (RS) Work 1 dc in 4th ch from hook, *skip 4 ch, shell in next ch; rep from *, end last rep skip 4 ch, 2 dc in last ch. Turn.
Row 2 Ch 3 (counts as 1 dc), skip first dc, 1 dc in next dc, *shell in center ch-1 sp of shell; rep from *, end 2 dc in top of t-ch. Turn.
Rep row 2.

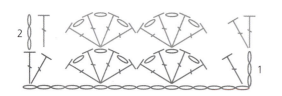

STITCH KEY
- ○ chain (ch)
- ╪ double crochet (dc)

75. Forward/Reverse

COLORS
A (golden yellow) and B (light pink)

Worked over multiple 2 sts plus 1.
Row 1 (RS) With A, ch 1, 1 sc in first and each st across. Fasten off. Do not turn.
Row 2 (RS) With B, working from left to right, ch 1, 1 sc in first sc, *ch 1, skip 1 sc, 1 sc in next sc; rep from * to end. Fasten off.

COLOR & STITCH KEY

- A ⬯ chain (ch)
- B + single crochet (sc)
- → direction of row

76. Spike Stitch Rolled

COLORS
A (orange) and B (light pink)

STITCH GLOSSARY
Spike sc Insert hook 2–3 rows down from edge, yo, draw up a lp and complete as for sc.

Worked over multiple of 2 sts plus 1.
Row 1 (RS) With A, ch 1, Spike sc in first st, *ch 1, skip 1 st, Spike sc in next st; rep from * evenly across. Fasten off.
Row 2 (RS) With B, ch 2 (counts as 1 hdc), skip first sc, *1 hdc in ch-1 sp, 1 hdc in back lp of sc; rep from * to end. Fasten off, leaving long tail for sewing.

ROLLED EDGING
Fold edge in half to WS. Using tail, sew front B loop to front A loop forming rolled edge.

COLOR & STITCH KEY

- A ⬯ chain (ch)
- B T half double crochet (hdc)   ∪ Spike single crochet (Spike sc)

77. Spike with Slip Stitch

COLORS
A (golden yellow) and B (orange)

STITCH GLOSSARY
Spike sc Insert hook 2–3 rows down from edge, yo, draw up a lp and complete as for sc.

Worked over multiple of 2 sts plus 1.
Row 1 (RS) With A, ch 1, Spike sc in next st, ch 1, skip next st; rep from *, end Spike sc in last st. Fasten off.
Row 2 (RS) With B, sl st through back loop in every st and ch. Fasten off.

COLOR & STITCH KEY

- A ⬯ chain (ch)
- B ∪ Spike single crochet (Spike sc)   · slip stitch through back loop (sl st tbl)

78. Modified Reverse Slip Stitch

Worked over multiple of 2 sts plus 1.
Row 1 (RS) Working from left to right, ch 1, *sl st in next st, ch 1, skip 1 st; rep from * evenly across, end sl st in last st.

STITCH KEY

◦ chain (ch)

• slip stitch (sl st)

→ direction of row

79. Single Crochet Slip Stitch

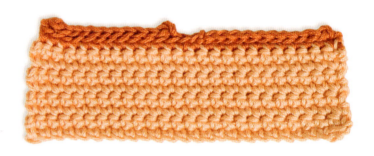

BOTH SIDES OF SAMPLE SWATCH
Worked over any multiple of sts plus 1.
Row 1 (RS) Ch 1, 1 sc in each st across. Fasten off.

RIGHT SIDE OF SAMPLE SWATCH
Row 2 (RS) Ch 1, sl st in each sc across.

LEFT SIDE OF SAMPLE SWATCH
Row 2 (RS) Ch 1, sl st through back loop of each sc across.

STITCH KEY

◦ chain (ch)

+ single crochet (sc)

• slip stitch (sl st)

⌒ slip stitch through back loop (sl st tbl)

80. Reverse Single Crochet Chain

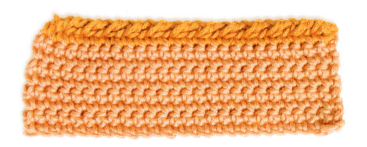

Worked over multiple of 2 sts plus 1.
Row 1 (RS) Ch 1, 1 sc in first and each st across. Do not turn.
Row 2 (RS) Ch 1, working from left to right, *1 sc in next sc, ch 1, skip 1 sc; rep from *, end 1 sc in last st. Fasten off.

STITCH KEY

◦ chain (ch)

+ single crochet (sc)

→ direction of rows

81. Reverse Half Double Crochet

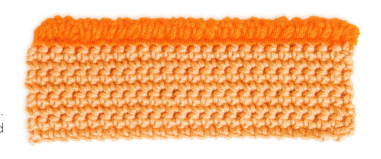

Worked over any multiple of sts plus 1.
Row 1 (RS) Ch 1, 1 sc in first and each st across. Do not turn.
Row 2 (RS) Ch 2, working from left to right, 1 hdc in first and each sc across. Fasten off.

STITCH KEY
◯ chain (ch)
✚ single crochet (sc)
T half double crochet (hdc)
→ direction of row

82. Double Crochet Corded

COLORS
A (golden yellow) and B (orange)

Worked over any multiple of sts.
Row 1 (RS) With A, ch 1, 1 sc in first and each st across. Do not turn.
Row 2 (RS) With B, ch 3, 1 dc in each sc across. Fasten off, leaving long tail for sewing.

CORDED EDGING
Fold edge in half to WS. Using tail, sew front lp of each dc and corresponding horizontal lp on sc row to form corded edge.

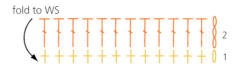

COLOR & STITCH KEY
▢ A   ◯ chain (ch)
▢ B   ✚ single crochet (sc)
        T double crochet (dc)

83. Chain Scallop

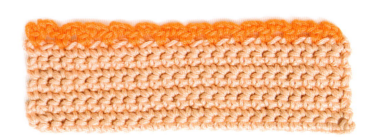

Worked over multiple of 2 sts plus 1.
Row 1 (RS) Ch 1, 1 sc in first st, *ch 3, skip 1 st, 1 sc in next st; rep from * evenly across. Fasten off.

STITCH KEY
◯ chain (ch)
✚ single crochet (sc)

84. Double Crochet Chain

Worked over any multiple of 2 sts plus 1.
Row 1 (RS) Ch 1, 1 sc in first and each st across. Fasten off. Do not turn.
Row 2 (RS) Ch 3, skip first sc, *1 dc in next sc, ch 1, skip 1 sc; rep from *, end 1 dc in last 2 sc. Fasten off.

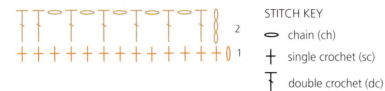

STITCH KEY
◦ chain (ch)
+ single crochet (sc)
⊤ double crochet (dc)

85. Tipsy Picot

STITCH GLOSSARY
Picot (3-ch) Ch 3, sl st in 3rd ch from hook.

Worked over multiple of 3 sts plus 2.
Row 1 (RS) Ch 1, 1 sc in first and each st across. Fasten off. Do not turn.
Row 2 (RS) Ch 1, 1 sc in first 3 sc, *Picot, 1 sc in next 3 sc; rep from *, end last rep 1 sc in last 2 sc. Fasten off.

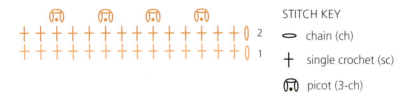

STITCH KEY
◦ chain (ch)
+ single crochet (sc)
⋒ picot (3-ch)

86. Chain Picot Edging

STITCH GLOSSARY
Picot (6-ch) Ch 6, sl st in 3rd ch from hook.

Row 1 (RS) Ch 1, 1 sc in edge, *picot, ch 3, skip approx 1"/2.5cm along edge, 1 sc in edge; rep from * evenly across. Fasten off.

STITCH KEY
◦ chain (ch)
+ single crochet (sc)
⋒ picot (6-ch)

87. Littlest Scallop

Worked over multiple of 2 sts plus 1.
Row 1 (RS) Ch 1, 1 sc in first and in each st across. Fasten off. Do not turn.
Row 2 (RS) Ch 1, (sl st, ch 3, 1 dc) in first sc, *skip 1 sc, (sl st, ch 3, 1 dc) in next sc; rep from * to end. Fasten off.

STITCH KEY
◯ chain (ch)
✚ single crochet (sc)
╤ double crochet (dc)
• slip stitch (sl st)

88. Picot Ruffle

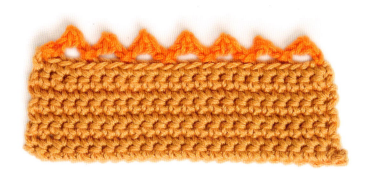

STITCH GLOSSARY
Picot (3-ch) Ch 3, 1 sc in 2nd ch from hook.

Worked over multiple of 3 sts plus 1.
Row 1 (RS) Sl st in back lp of first st, *Picot, ch 1, skip 2 sts, sl st in back lp of next st; rep from * to end. Fasten off.

STITCH KEY
◯ chain (ch)
✚ single crochet (sc)
⌒ sl st in back lp

89. Wuffle Ruffle

STITCH GLOSSARY
Picot (4-ch) Ch 4, 1 sc in 4th ch from hook.

Worked over multiple of 4 sts plus 1.
Row 1 (RS) Ch 1, 1 sc in first and each st across. Fasten off. Do not turn.
Row 2 (RS) Ch 1, (1 sc, Picot, 1 sc) in first sc, *picot, skip 1 sc, 1 sc in next sc, Picot, skip 1 sc, (1 sc, Picot, 1 sc) in next sc; rep from * to end. Fasten off.

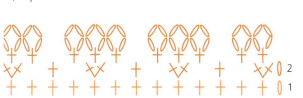

STITCH KEY
◯ chain (ch)
✚ single crochet (sc)
⬡ picot (4-ch)

90. Scallop Shell

Worked over multiple of 4 sts plus 1.
Row 1 (RS) Ch 1, 1 sc in first and each st across. Fasten off. Do not turn.
Row 2 (RS) Ch 1, 1 sc in first sc, *skip 1 sc, 5 dc in next sc, skip 1 sc, 1 sc in next sc; rep from * to end. Fasten off.

STITCH KEY
⊖ chain (ch)
+ single crochet (sc)
T double crochet (dc)

91. Pearl Shell

STITCH GLOSSARY
CL (3-dc cluster) 3 dc in same st.

Worked over multiple of 6 sts plus 1.
Row 1 (RS) Ch 1, 1 sc in first and each st across. Fasten off. Do not turn.
Row 2 (RS) Ch 1, 1 sc in first 3 sc, *3 sc in next sc, 1 sc in next 5 sc; rep from *, end last rep 1 sc in last 3 sc. Fasten off. Do not turn.
Row 3 (RS) Ch 3, skip 3 sc, *CL in center st of next 3-sc group, ch 2, skip 2 sc, 1 sc in next sc, ch 2, skip 2 sc; rep from *, end CL in center sc of last 3-sc group, ch 2, skip 2 sc, 1 sc in last sc. Fasten off.

STITCH KEY
⊖ chain (ch)
+ single crochet (sc)
⋎ 3-double crochet cluster (CL)

92. Little Scallop

Worked over multiple of 3 sts plus 1.
Row 1 (RS) Ch 1, 1 sc in first and each st across. Fasten off. Do not turn.
Row 2 (RS) Ch 1, (1 sc, 1 dc, ch 1, 1 dc, 1 sc) in first sc, *skip 2 sc, (1 sc, 1 dc, ch 1, 1 dc, 1 sc) in next sc; rep from * to end. Fasten off.

STITCH KEY
⊖ chain (ch)
+ single crochet (sc)
T double crochet (dc)

93. Ruffled Shell

STITCH GLOSSARY
CL3 (3-dc shell) 3 dc in same st.
CL5 (5-dc shell) 5 dc in same st.

Worked over multiple of 6 sts plus 1.
Row 1 (WS) Ch 1, 1 sc in first and each st across. Turn.
Row 2 (RS) Ch 3, CL3 in first sc, *1 sc in next sc, skip 1 sc, CL5 in next sc, skip 1 sc, 1 sc in next sc, CL5 in sc; rep from *, end last rep CL3 in last sc. Turn.
Row 3 Ch 1, 1 sc in first dc, skip 2 dc, *CL5 in next sc, skip 2 dc, 1 sc in 3rd dc of CL5; rep from *, end last rep 1 sc in 3rd dc of CL3. Fasten off.

STITCH KEY
⚬ chain (ch)
✚ single crochet (sc)
╪ double crochet (dc)

94. Classic Shell

Worked over multiple of 6 sts plus 1.
Row 1 (RS) Ch 1, 1 sc in first and each st across. Fasten off. Do not turn.
Row 2 (RS) Ch 1, 1 sc in first sc, *skip 2 sc, 5 dc in next sc, skip 2 sc, 1 sc in next sc; rep from * to end. Fasten off.

STITCH KEY
⚬ chain (ch)
✚ single crochet (sc)
╪ double crochet (dc)

95. String of Pearls

COLORS
A (golden yellow) and B (light pink)

Worked over multiple of 3 sts.
Row 1 (RS) With A, ch 1, 1 sc in first and each st across. Fasten off. Do not turn.
Row 2 (RS) With A, rep row 1. Fasten off. Do not turn.
Row 3 (RS) With B, *sl st in next 2 sc, (sl st, ch 3, 1 dc, ch 3, sl st) in next sc; rep from * to end. Fasten off.

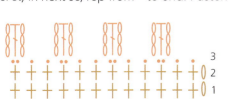

COLOR & STITCH KEY
▪ A ⚬ chain (ch)
▪ B ✚ single crochet (sc)
• slip stitch (sl st)
╪ double crochet (dc)

96. Spike with Chain Loops

COLORS
A (light orange) and B (golden yellow)

STITCH GLOSSARY
Spike sc Insert hook approx 1"/2.5cm down from edge, yo, draw up a lp and complete as for sc.

Worked over multiple of 12 sts plus 2.
Row 1 (RS) With A, ch 1, *Spike sc in next st, ch 1, sl st in next st, ch 1; rep from * evenly across, end Spike sc in last st. Fasten off. Do not turn.
Row 2 (RS) With B, ch 1, 1 sc in first st, *ch 4, skip 2 sts, 1 sc in next st; rep from *, end 1 sc in last st. Fasten off.

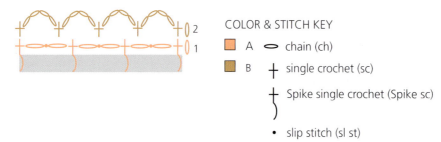

COLOR & STITCH KEY

- A — chain (ch)
- B + single crochet (sc)
- Spike single crochet (Spike sc)
- • slip stitch (sl st)

97. Spike and Chain Frill

COLORS
A (light pink) and B (golden yellow)

STITCH GLOSSARY
Spike sc Insert hook 2–3 rows down from edge, yo, draw up a lp and complete as for sc.
Frill (1 Sc, ch 4, 1 sl st, ch 4, 1 sc) in same st.

Worked over multiple of 6 sts plus 1.
Row 1 (RS) With A, ch 1, Spike sc in first st, *ch 4, skip 2 sts, Spike sc in next st; rep from * to end. Fasten off. Do not turn.
Row 2 (RS) With B, ch 1, (1 sc, ch 2, 1 sc) in first st, *ch 2, skip ch-4 sp, Frill in next sc, ch 2, skip ch-4 sp, (1 sc, ch 2, 1 sc) in next sc; rep from * to end. Fasten off.

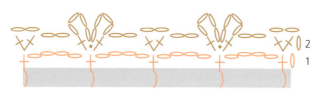

COLOR & STITCH KEY

- A — chain (ch)
- B + single crochet (sc)
- double crochet (dc)
- Spike single crochet (Spike sc)

98. Double Half Double with Picot

COLORS
A (light pink) and B (orange)

STITCH GLOSSARY
Picot (3-ch) Ch 3, sl st in 3rd ch from hook.

Worked over multiple of 5 sts plus 2.
Row 1 (RS) With A, ch 2, 1 hdc in first st, *skip 1 st, 2 hdc in next st; rep from * evenly across. Fasten off. Do not turn.
Row 2 (RS) With B, ch 1, 1 sc in first hdc, *Picot, 1 sc in next 4 hdc; rep from *, end Picot, 1 sc in last 2 hdc. Fasten off.

COLOR & STITCH KEY
- A — chain (ch)
- B — single crochet (sc)
- half double crochet (hdc)
- Picot (3-ch)

99. Chain and Zigzag

COLORS
A (golden yellow) and B (orange)

STITCH GLOSSARY
Chain st Insert hook into work approx ½"/1.3cm from edge, yo and draw lp to RS and through lp on hook.

Row 1 (RS) With A, working parallel to edge, make a slipknot, place on hook and hold yarn at WS, chain st evenly across. Fasten off. Do not turn.
Row 2 (RS) With B, make a slipknot, place on hook and hold yarn at WS, *(insert hook to WS then back to RS of work below chain, yo and draw up lp to RS, complete as for sc), ch 2, (insert hook to WS then back to RS of work in an angle above chain, yo and draw up lp to RS, complete as for sc), ch 2; rep from * evenly across, end 1 sc below chain st. Fasten off.

COLOR & STITCH KEY
- A — chain (ch)
- B — single crochet (sc)

100. Crown Point

STITCH GLOSSARY
Bobble (3-tr) [Yo twice, insert hook into st, yo and draw up a lp, (yo and draw through 2 lps on hook) twice] 3 times, yo and draw through all 4 lps on hook.
Picot (3-ch) Ch 3, sl st in 3rd ch from hook.

Worked over multiple of 7 sts.
Row 1 (RS) Ch 3, 1 dc in next and each st across. Fasten off. Do not turn.
Row 2 (RS) Ch 1, 1 sc in first dc, *ch 5, Bobble in next dc, Picot, skip 3 dc, Bobble in next dc, ch 5, 1 sc in next 2 dc; rep from *, end last rep, 1 sc in last dc. Fasten off.

STITCH KEY

⌒ chain

+ single crochet (sc)

⊤ double crochet (dc)

◆ 3-treble cluster (bobble)

⌒ picot (3-ch)

101. Shells and Columns

Worked over multiple of 10 sts plus 6.
Row 1 (RS) Ch 1, 1 sc in first and each st across. Turn.
Row 2 Ch 3, skip first sc, 1 dc in next sc, *ch 1, skip 1 sc, 1 dc in next 2 sc; rep from * to end. Turn.
Row 3 Ch 3, skip first dc, 1 dc in each dc and each ch-1 sp across, end 1 dc in top of t-ch. Turn.
Rep rows 2 and 3 if longer edging is desired.
Row 4 Ch 3, skip first 2 dc, *2 dc in next dc, ch 2, 2 dc in next dc, ch 1, skip 3 dc; rep from *, end last rep skip 1 dc, 1 dc in top of t-ch. Turn.
Row 5 Ch 1, *skip 2 dc, 7 dc in ch-2 sp, skip (2 dc, ch 1, 2 dc), 1 sc in next ch-2 sp; rep from *, end skip 2 dc, 7 dc in last ch-2 sp, skip 2 dc, 1 sc in top of t-ch. Fasten off.

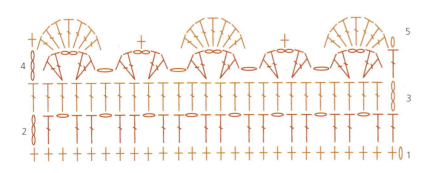

STITCH KEY

⌒ chain (ch)

+ single crochet (sc)

⊤ double crochet (dc)